Jersey Shore

Haunted
Jersey Shore

Ghosts and Strange Phenomena
of the Garden State Coast

Charles A. Stansfield Jr.
Illustrations by Heather Adel Wiggins

STACKPOLE
BOOKS

Published by
STACKPOLE BOOKS
5067 Ritter Road
Mechanicsburg, PA 17055
www.stackpolebooks.com

Printed in the United States of America

10 9 8 7 6 5 4 3

FIRST EDITION

Design by Beth Oberholtzer
Cover design by Caroline Stover

Library of Congress Cataloging-in-Publication Data

Stansfield, Charles A.
    Haunted Jersey shore: ghosts and strange phenomena of the Garden State coast / Charles A. Stansfield, Jr. ; illustrations by Heather Adel Wiggins.-1st ed.
        p.   cm.
    Includes bibliographical references.
    ISBN-13: 978-0-8117-3267-3 (pbk.)
    ISBN-10: 0-8117-3267-3 (pbk.)
    1. Ghosts-New Jersey   2. Haunted places-New Jersey.   I. Title.
BF1472.U6S725   2006
133.1'09749'09146-dc22   2005019596

In loving memory of my grandparents,
Thomas and Christine,
and Walter and Alice;
and to all who have traveled
in search of light.

Contents

Introduction 1
   Superstitions of the Sea 6
   Water-Dwelling Monsters 9

North Shore 11
   The Pirates Who Came Back to New Jersey 11
   The Ghosts of the *Morro Castle* 12
   Get Out! Get Out! 14
   Captain Huddy's Ghost 16
   A Presidential Ghost 18
   The End of an Era 19
   The Ghost in the Library 20
   The Spy House and Its Many Ghosts 22
   The Lady Who Didn't Want to Leave 23
   The Devil and the Drunkard 23
   The Lost Explorer 24
   Penelope's Nightmare Honeymoon 25
   The Ghostly Noah's Ark 26
   The Wrestling Match on the Beach 27
   The Captain and the Pigeon 28
   The Indian Who Refused to Go Along 29
   Molly Still Brings the Pitcher 30

Central Shore 33
   The Hoodoo Schooner 33
   Still Following the North Star 34
   Bringing Home the Bacon 35
   Parental Love Never Dies 36
   The Jersey Shore's Most Famous Ghost 37
   Help! Shark! 39
   Looking for Pirates' Trees 40
   The Lighthouse Builder's Ghost 40
   The Lighthouse Keeper's Ghost 41
   The Ghost of the Airship 42
   The Phantom Canal Diggers 44
   The Old Seadog's Ghost 46
   The Ghosts Drink to St. Francis 47
   The Ghost Beacons of the Tuckerton Tower 48
   The Sailing Ship on Rails 49
   New Jersey's "Paul Revere" 49

South Shore 51
   The Ghost with the Most Diamonds 51
   Taps at the Cape May Point Bunker 52
   The Ghost Who Is So Proud 53
   The Haunted Cottage 54
   Reasoning with the Ghost 55
   Reliving Bessie's Happiest Evening 56
   The Phantom Lifeguard 57
   The Helpful Little Dog 58
   The Ghost of the Tragic Chambermaid 59
   The Ghost in the Elephant 59
   Heading Back to a Safe Harbor 60
   The Case of the Terrified Cat 61
   The Ghost Who Loves to Tango 62
   King Nummy's Mummy 63
   The Ghostly Tap Dancer 64
   The Witch and the Lizard 65
   The Colonel's Ghostly Inspection Tours 66
   The Peace-Loving Ghost of Cape May 67
   Captain Kidd's Brigantine Treasure 68
   Pirate Ghosts at Cape May Point 69

Contents

The Ghosts of Absecon Lighthouse 71
A Room with a View 72

The Pinelands 75
The Wizard of the Pines 75
The Wreck of the Blue Comet 76
The Jersey Devil Has Company 78
The Legend of the Jersey Devil 79
The Bottomless "Blue Hole" 83
Are Ghost Sightings a Symptom of "Apple Palsy"? 84
Ghost Towns of the Pinelands 84
The Dancing Bandit 85
Fiddling with the Devil 87

Northern Tidewater 89
The Ghost of the Traitor General 89
The Ghost of Mary Rogers 90
The Ghost of Washington's Spy 91
Jimmy Hoffa's Ghost Cheers Them On 92
The Triple Airship Still Flies 93
The Poetic Ghost from Matawan 94

Delaware Bay and River 97
The Town Named for a Disaster 97
Stretch Garrison Rides Again 97
Blood Money 98
The Confederate Ghosts of Finn's Point 99
The Youngest Confederate Ghost 101
Thar She Blows, There She Goes 102
The Hanged Pirate 102
The Doomed Ferryboat 103
The "Big Tub" in the Little Tub 103
Ghostly Perfumed Smoke 104

Ghost Tours on the Haunted Jersey Shore 107
Getting Weird on the Jersey Shore 109
Bibliography 111
Acknowledgments 113
About the Author 115

Introduction

THE JERSEY SHORE—THAT GLORIOUS STRAND OF BEACHES FROM SANDY Hook in the north to Cape May in the south—is haunted. The great bays and rivers flanking the beaches on both north and south are haunted as well. Just behind the seashore, the infamous Pine Barrens have their share of supernatural phenomena, from ghost towns to grisly murders to witchcraft. New Jersey's "official state demon"—the Jersey Devil—is one of the many weird apparitions that frequent both Pinelands and seashore locales.

This book brings together stories and traditions of ghosts, witches, monsters, and other strange phenomena from the seashore and neighboring Pinelands and Tidewater vicinities. The book is organized into regions: the Northern Shore, from Sandy Hook to Barnegat; the Central Shore, Long Beach Island; the Southern Shore, from Brigantine to Cape May; the neighboring Pinelands, fringing the seashore; the Northern Tidewater, consisting of Sandy Hook, Raritan, Newark and New York Bays, and the Hudson and Hackensack Rivers; and the Southern Tidewater, encompassing Delaware Bay and River. All of these regions share the mystical, spirit-attracting qualities of water. In so many instances, ghosts seem to be almost magnetically drawn to the shores and banks of water features. It is not at all surprising that ghost stories from the Jersey Shore often involve shipwrecks, pirates, lighthouses, and sailors.

As a geographer, I have come to realize that ghost stories have a geography: They relate to specific places and reflect the regions' physical, economic, and cultural geography. Also, ghosts themselves have a very specific geography: They almost always are territorial and haunt a particular building, usually just a room in the building. The ghost associated with a haunted house, for example, never shows up in a neighbor's house or wanders down the street to the convenience store.

Most of the stories in this book will be new to the majority of readers. In the interest of completeness, however, a few classic Jersey Shore ghost stories that appeared in my previous volume, *Haunted New Jersey: Ghosts and Strange Phenomena of the Garden State*, such as those of Captain Huddy and the Woman in White, have also been included here, although often in different versions of the same basic story.

Ask any beachgoer about the Jersey Shore, and it's unlikely that he or she will talk about anything except the sandy beaches, the ocean waves, and the large number of people who flock there each summer. The happy resort image of New Jersey's seashore, with sun-filled days of innocent fun in this realm of sand and surf, stands in sharp contrast to its place in the spirit world. But the 127 mile-long string of beaches also has a dark side—a shadowy world of greed, violent death, betrayal, and murder—with a number of tragic shipwrecks, the murderous actions of wreckers who lured ships into dangerously shallow waters, and many visits by ruthless pirates to these shores.

Was it an omen that the first two explorers to see the Jersey Shore, Giovanni da Verrazano and Henry Hudson, had very bad luck afterward? Verrazano was the first European known to have viewed the Jersey beaches—from a distance. Rather than attempting to land here, he sailed along the coast in 1524 and claimed the area for his employers, the French. But they took no practical steps to take possession of the region, which to them was unimpressive. Verrazano was later captured, killed, and eaten by cannibals in the Caribbean.

It wasn't until 1609, eighty-five years later, that another explorer bothered to sail along New Jersey's shores. Like Verrazano, Henry Hudson was not especially excited about the seashore and didn't get off the boat to look at it. Later, while exploring his namesake bay in Canada, his boat was locked in ice over the winter. His crew mutinied and set him adrift in a small boat come spring, while they sailed for home. Hudson was never heard from again.

Few now are aware of the first impressions of the early explorers, who saw little good and much to fear as they surveyed the coast between the Hudson and Delaware Rivers. Henry Hudson noted that the waves broke over shallow, submerged sandbars many yards off the beaches, and that the inlets or channels between the islands along the southern shores were narrow, twisting, and only a few feet deep—not a welcoming shoreline for sailors. Like other seafarers before and since, Hudson was favorably impressed not with New Jersey's coast, but with the great natural harbors that flanked it to the north and south. The broad, sandy beaches sloping gently into the waves allow vacationers to wade out into the surf for the thrill of braving the breakers. But the same qualities that make New Jersey's ocean shoreline a great natural playground also made it, for centuries, a death trap. Very shallow water, breaking waves, and the low, flat horizon of most of the seashore made this a hostile shoreline for early sailors—except, that is, for those who flew the skull and crossbones.

Because of the great number of shipwrecks along the New Jersey shorelines, some of the first, tallest, and most famous lighthouses in the country are found here. And the first federal government–sponsored lifesaving stations were built along the Jersey coast. This "graveyard of the Atlantic," as it became known to early seafarers, has become as haunted as other graveyards. No one really knows how many victims of shipwrecks lie restlessly on the seabed, their bones tossed about like seashells by waves and currents, their spirits condemned to wander the sands.

Was the dreadful loss of life, and the resultant hauntings of the Jersey beaches, the motive for the establishment of a chain of federal lifesaving stations along the shore? Many people thought so at the time. The restless spirits of drowned sailors and the ships' passengers have haunted virtually every seaside community. It is said that ghosts are particularly active when they are not resigned to their fate, when their deaths were not the result of true accidents but were caused by criminals. Two varieties of mass murderers visited New Jersey beaches in times past: wreckers and pirates.

Wreckers caused many shipwreck disasters along the coast by luring ships onto the sandbars and beaches in order to loot their cargoes and strip dead bodies of valuables. It started innocently enough. People living near the then isolated beaches were in the habit of beachcombing for anything useful that might wash up on their doorsteps. Shipwrecks were a bonanza for beachcombers, who salvaged the abandoned cargoes and often sold them at auction. "Finders, keepers" was the rule. Many a wrecked ship's timbers were used to build houses, furniture, and fences ashore.

There was nothing wrong with recycling these gifts of the sea when they were the products of natural disasters. The problem came when a few locals, lured by the prospects of easy pickings, decided not only to take advantage of shipwrecks, but to cause them. In the days before most lighthouses had been built, ships cruising along the coast had few clues as to exactly where the shoreline was at night. Jersey had a very low-profile shore, with few houses or landmarks. On moonless or stormy nights, wreckers would tie a lantern to the tail of a donkey or horse and lead the animal slowly along the beach. The light, swinging slightly from the creature's tail and making slow progress parallel to the shipping lanes, was a good imitation of a ship's riding light, swinging back and forth with the sway of a ship under sail. The crews of ships at sea, seeing the light of what appeared to be another ship, would misjudge the actual distance to the shore and thus venture into shallow waters and be grounded on the sands. Unable to maneuver or break free, the ships were pounded by the surf and broke up, with cargo, sailors, and passengers alike spilling into the sea.

Even after the first lighthouses were built on the Jersey coast, the wreckers still provided false information to ships at sea. They would walk a lighted lantern around and around a tall haystack built on the beach, so that the disappearing and reappearing beam would resemble the revolving light atop a lighthouse.

Many lives were sacrificed to the greed of the wreckers, who sometimes were also called pirates or "mooncussers" (moon cursers), the latter because they were said to have "cussed" the full moon, the light of which helped navigators avoid danger. The wreckers were much more interested in salvaging cargo than in rescuing people. The dead who washed ashore were stripped of jewelry, money, and even clothing, then left unburied.

Pirates. The word sent shivers through the civilized world between the seventeenth and nineteenth centuries. The merciless buccaneers terrorized sailing ships and coastal towns, and they frequented the Jersey shoreline because it offered numerous opportunities. Here was a lonely coast with few to notice or report the presence of unfamiliar ships or sailors. It was close to busy ports,

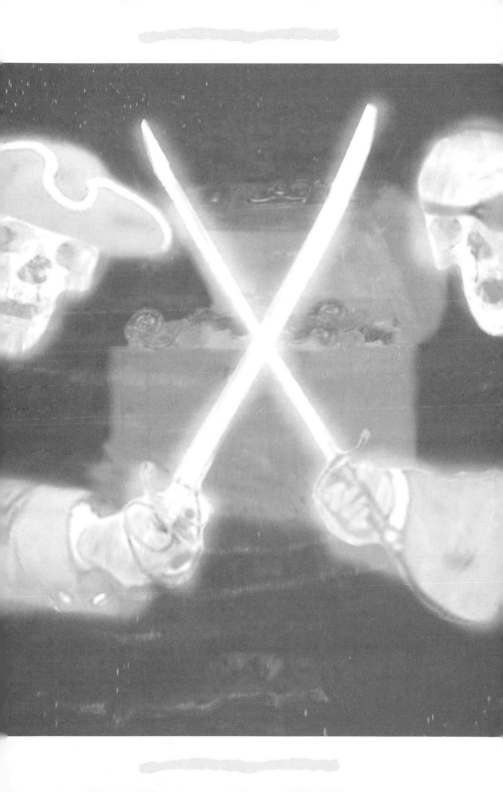

with many valuable cargoes going to or coming from other ports around the world—temptations for bloodthirsty pirates.

But pirates thirsted for more than blood and treasure. Like all sailors, they needed to land on occasion to replenish their supplies of fresh water. Not wanting to risk entering ports in search of water, the pirates preferred to land in isolated, uninhabited places to refill their water casks. A freshwater spring called the "spout" on Sandy Hook became a favorite of pirates, including the notorious Captain Kidd. At the opposite end of the Jersey Shore, freshwater Lake Lily at Cape May Point was another pirate watering hole that also attracted Kidd's attention.

Woe to any local residents who might stumble into a pirate crew landing for water. Witnesses were killed immediately. It is widely believed that pirates sometimes buried treasure near their water sources, intending to dig them up again in the future. The usual suspects among pirates said to have left treasure in New Jersey include Jean Lafitte of New Orleans, Blackbeard (a.k.a. Edward Teach), and Captain Kidd. Alleged burial sites ran along the seacoast from Sandy Hook to Cape May Point, and inland up the Delaware, Mullica, Maurice, Cohansey, and Great Egg Harbor Rivers. There are rumors of buried treasure on Sandy Hook, Money Island, Long Beach Island, and Cape May Point.

Superstitions of the Sea

Sailors and fishermen know firsthand the dangers and mysteries of the sea. Most are firm believers in luck, both good and bad, and superstitions of the sea form an ancient tradition of omens, avoidances, warnings, and beliefs that guide their behavior.

New Jersey has a long history of sailors and fishermen. Those who are brave enough to go to sea share many superstitions about how to behave at sea and how to read the signs of good or bad luck. The word *superstition* comes from a Latin word meaning "soothsaying." Soothsayers foretold the future, and they were supposed to foretell it accurately, as *sooth* means the truth or reality. For sailing ships, the Jersey coast was a dangerous place to avoid at all costs; safe harbors were on the Hudson and Delaware Rivers. Ships need not only protected harbors, but also deep water alongside land, and these requirements were not found between Sandy

Hook on the north and Cape May to the south. The winds that carried ships across the seas could also smash them against the shore. Ships were safest either far at sea, where no land existed, or in deep-water harbors protecting them from storm waves. Sailing vessels tried to stay well off New Jersey's treacherously shallow shoreline of gentle beaches and deceptive inlets. But given the busy ports at either end of the Jersey coast, this hostile shore was not always easily avoided. Many ships in the vicinity, shallow waters, and frequent storms all added up to make this the graveyard of the Atlantic.

Those who made a living on the waves were very vulnerable, and as a result, they were interested in avoiding bad luck and inviting good luck. The superstitions familiar to many sailors and fishermen are ancient, but they are still observed today along the shores and on the waters of New Jersey.

If a crewmember or passenger died aboard ship, this was considered a very bad omen. By tradition, the body was carefully handled and disposed of, lest the ghost stay aboard. The corpse had to be laid parallel to the ship's keel, lengthwise not crosswise. The head had to be at the back so that as the ghost rose from the body, it would face the bow, in the direction the ship was traveling. If the ship was more than a day from port, the body had to be buried at sea. On a sailing ship, the corpse was sewn into a sail before being dumped overboard. The body was weighted so that it would sink before it attracted sharks.

It was believed that a ship should always be boarded right foot first, and from the ship's right (starboard) side. Although some old-timers thought that a woman aboard might bring bad luck, all agreed that a baby being born aboard brought good luck to that ship. When a ship embarked on its first voyage, an old shoe would be thrown into its wake, much like tying old shoes to the car of a couple departing on their honeymoon. Seasoned sailors tossed a penny overboard as their ship left its dock, a tribute to Neptune, god of the sea. If Neptune didn't get his tribute, he might have seen to it that the ship never returned. Similarly, to guarantee a good catch, fishermen tossed a penny into the first net to be lowered to appease Neptune. Some said that tossing a little salt into the sea would produce a good catch. Many fishermen tossed back the first fish caught on the voyage to encourage Neptune to send more fish toward them. On a fishing boat's first voyage, however, the first fish caught was nailed to the mast.

A ship under construction was never called by its name. The name was officially known only at launching. For this reason, ship-yards assign a number to "builds" or "hulls" under construction. The number refers to the hull's sequence among all boats or ships built there, as in "Hull 121" or "Build 98." Once named at launch-ing, it was considered very bad luck to ever change the name. Even if a male name was given, a ship was always referred to as "she."

The custom of smashing a bottle of champagne against the bow of a ship, often called "christening," has its origins in a dark super-stition of the Vikings. The ancient warriors always launched their longboats over the bodies of enemies or slaves so that the boat slid into the sea easily, having been lubricated by blood. A boat "born in blood" would have a long, lucky life, riding high over the waves. In less bloodthirsty times, red wine was substituted for blood, and eventually champagne was used. It is considered bad luck if the champagne bottle does not break on the first contact with the ship. To avoid such bad luck, experienced boat builders supply a bottle that has been scratched or incised in several places to encourage easy breaking.

European sailors believe that a cat aboard ship is good luck, but two cats bring bad luck. If the cat falls overboard, the ship may be doomed. American sailors have mixed opinions on cats aboard ship; some think they are good luck, but others think cats bring bad luck.

There are many seafarer superstitions about birds. Bringing a live bird aboard in a cage is the worst luck. But if a bird lands on a ship at sea, it is usually good luck. If a land-based bird, like a spar-row or robin, lands aboard, it is an honored guest seeking refuge and brings good luck. An albatross, thought to contain a dead sea-man's spirit, must never be killed. Its very appearance heralds a storm. Bird droppings on deck must not be removed until after the next storm, which will most likely remove them anyway. Seagulls may bring bad luck; they are believed to contain the restless spirits of those drowned at sea. When gulls fly in a long, straight line over the water, they are following a drowned man's spirit moving across the seabed. Though not welcomed, gulls must never be harmed.

Truly superstitious sailors may believe that a seabird defecating on them is the best fortune of all.

Sea creatures also feature in many superstitions. A shark following a boat foretells a death aboard; three sharks trailing a boat practically guarantee impending death. Porpoises or dolphins are good news. Considered friendly to people, porpoises are said to welcome lucky ships into a harbor. Porpoises at play during a storm foretell a quick end to that storm. Whales generally are good omens, but seeing a whale in a place where they have not been seen before could be a bad omen. Seeing whales "out of season" (on New Jersey's coast, whales are "in season" during winter) could signify bad news.

If a fisherman, on his way to the harbor, comes across a member of the clergy, a cross-eyed person, or a woman wearing a white apron, he should go home and not board his vessel until the next tide. It is very unlucky to take the name of the Almighty in vain while at sea.

When building a ship, a silver coin must be placed under the base of a mast. Failure to do so will mean the mast will fall in a storm. It is bad luck to paint a ship green.

Davy Jones is an evil spirit believed to live at the bottom of the sea. It is thought that Davy is a West Indian voodoo name for the Devil, and that the Welsh surname Jones is derived from Jonah, the biblical name that must never be given a future sailor or fisherman.

Water-Dwelling Monsters

Water-dwelling monsters hold an especially terrifying fascination because we can't see them, at least not until it is clearly too late. What we can't see, we can't understand. And what we don't understand, we fear. Since the early Colonial period, people have reported strange creatures dwelling in the Delaware River and the Atlantic Ocean off the New Jersey coast.

The Swedes who pioneered in the Delaware Valley during the seventeenth century claimed that they saw at least two different river monsters. It is said that the local Indians called these beasts Manitto, or "Devil-fish." One type was described as a headless, boneless mass of jellylike or spongy substance. It could project its bowels outward quickly to envelop a fish, surrounding its prey and then sucking it into its shapeless body. A second type was a more serpentlike monster with the head of a dog. This one could sever a man's leg in one bite. It could allegedly swim much faster than a man and could hurl itself ashore to catch an unwary fisherman on the banks.

The waters off the Jersey shoreline have many tales and legends of monsters. And real monsters—sharks—do cruise these waters. Two recent books, Michael Capuzzo's *Close to Shore* and Richard Fernicola's *Twelve Days of Terror*, document the great New Jersey shore panic of 1916. In July of that year, a shark killed a bather at Beach Haven, and five days later, another victim died at Spring Lake. Six days after that, a shark entered the Matawan Creek, a tidal stream draining into the Raritan River, killing two more and seriously injuring a third. Many believe that the same shark—probably a great white—was responsible for all five attacks. At least one ghost still warns would-be swimmers that there were real sharks—hungry and aggressive sharks—behind the legends.

Many believe that the ghost that haunts Matawan is that of Lester Stillwell, whose life was so tragically cut short by New Jersey's true-life "Jaws." Rowboats on the still waters may suddenly be flipped if they foolishly venture into deep waters. Childish handwriting mysteriously appears on waterside docks, warning people not to go swimming. When adventurous local boys walk onto the bridge at night, planning a quick dip without their parent's knowledge, the ghost of a small boy appears to warn them off. Some claim to have heard a boy screaming out on the water, but no one is there.

North Shore

The Pirates Who Came Back to New Jersey

When Captain Kidd and his crew tried for piracy in London, the verdict was guilty. Kidd and most of his crew were hanged. In fact, Kidd was hanged twice. On the first attempt, the rope broke. Kidd claimed that this was a sign from God to spare his life. The hangman claimed it was a sign to use a stronger rope. The second attempt succeeded. But a few of those who sailed with the notorious pirate were not convicted. They had a good point in their defense—they were just following orders. The three sailors who were freed by the court had been apprenticed to the captain, and under English law, apprentices were legally bound to serve their master. Disobedience would result in severe punishment. What could they do? They were bound to follow Kidd's orders, like it or not. The court agreed.

At least two of Kidd's surviving crew returned to New Jersey to look for hidden treasure. It was well known that Captain Kidd, like other pirates, had a habit of burying treasure chests in remote places accessible to the sea, planning to retrieve them later. Pirates, who liked to call themselves the "brethren of the coast," had no honor among themselves. Sailors on pirate ships were understandably reluctant to go ashore on treasure-burying expeditions, because it was common for captains to kill sailors who helped bury their treasures. Dead men tell no tales. They don't come back and dig up the treasure for themselves, either.

It was rumored that Captain Kidd had buried treasure in several places along New Jersey's shoreline. And now, conveniently, Kidd was dead, and his surviving crew had some good ideas as to where to search for the treasure, so a pair of them came back to New Jersey on a treasure hunt. It seems likely that one of Kidd's apprentices did find treasure, but the spirit of the other is still looking. One, William Leeds, became a faithful member at Christ Episcopal Church in Shrewsbury. The church records state that Leeds was baptized there on October 20, 1702, a year after Kidd and most of his crew were hanged back in England. A man of leisure with no known source of income, Leeds contributed generously to the church. When he died, Leeds left his entire estate to the church. Among his possessions was a big chest, four feet long and two and a half feet deep. Careful examination revealed a hidden compartment, which turned out to hold nothing but dust. Some claim to have seen the ghost of Leeds sitting on his own grave in the churchyard. He appears to be counting gold coins as he stares at the church that the reformed pirate helped build with some of Captain Kidd's ill-gotten treasure.

The other, William Jenkins, changed his name to William Bennet and settled along the Barnegat bayshore at a place now known as Bennet's Neck. He lived as a hermit, discouraging any visitors. Bennet often was seen digging along the shores with a clam rake and shovel, but he never seemed to find any clams. And some of the holes he dug were much too deep for clamming. Was he digging for treasure? It is believed that the old pirate never found any treasure, for ever since he died, mysterious lantern lights have been seen along the nighttime shores as the old treasure hunter still digs secretly at night for the hidden treasure.

The Ghosts of the Morro Castle

New Jersey's most recent maritime disaster, the terrible fire that swept through the luxury cruise ship *Morro Castle*, occurred on September 7, 1934. But the ghosts of many of the victims of this long-ago tragedy have been known to prowl Jersey's beaches from Sea Girt to Asbury Park. The ghostly image of the burning ship has been sighted as well, both from the beaches and from ships at sea.

Some of the 134 passengers who perished died on the red-hot decks of the burning ship; others drowned after leaping into the stormy night ocean to escape the flames. When the still-burning hulk of the 508-foot-long liner drifted onto the beach just yards from the Asbury Park Convention Hall, it became a kind of bizarre, gruesome tourist attraction. Special excursion trains from Philadelphia and New York brought ghoulish crowds to gape at the disaster. In what may still hold the state record for a traffic jam, rubberneckers caused a monumental backup all the way from Asbury Park to the Holland Tunnel. An estimated 150,000 people came to see the ship of death.

In an eerie coincidence, the *Morro Castle* disaster was not only prophesied, but actually wished for. In author Hal Burton's story of this classic case of death at sea, *Morro Castle*, he quotes an 1884 editorial in the Asbury Park newspaper as stating: "We need a first-class shipwreck . . . to make Asbury Park a famous winter resort. The unlucky ship should strike head-on and we could accommodate her all winter."

Exactly that happened, and Asbury Park merchants had their most profitable week in years. Local businesspeople hurried to their banks with large deposits even as corpses were still being collected on the beaches.

The ghosts of the victims, and the ghost of the ship itself, may have lingered so long because the tragedy never should have happened. The *Morro Castle* was only a few years old and had been built to the latest standards of safety, including sprinkler systems to fight fire. The ship was a potential troopship in waiting, and her construction had been subsidized and overseen by the U.S. Navy, so her safety equipment was entirely up-to-date.

But the crew had not been drilled in emergency response. Mysteriously, the ship's captain was found dead in his cabin hours before fire broke out, and no "SOS" was sent for hours after the flames were first seen. Most investigators were convinced that arson was the cause of the loss of the ship and so many lives. That senseless criminal act alone could have produced the restless, vengeful spirits of the dead who still haunt Jersey's beaches.

Late on stormy nights, a flaming ship is sighted off the Monmouth County seashore resorts, sailing north toward New York, the home port that the *Morro Castle* never reached. But the ship does not exist, and on the beaches, the charred dead—or rather, the charred undead—can still be seen in spirit.

Perhaps Asbury Park's people learned one thing: In desiring a unique tourist attraction, be careful what you wish for.

Get Out! Get Out!

This particular incident happened more than sixty years ago to one very frightened victim. It is not known how many other appearances this ghost may have made over the years.

It was the early days of World War II. The newlyweds barely had time to settle into their little apartment before the husband joined the Navy. Soon he was on his way to a ship in the Pacific. His wife's parents recently had rented an old house in Long Branch and suggested that their daughter move in with them, as they had plenty of room. The young woman, whom we'll call Eleanor, moved into a second-floor bedroom, which after a few weeks proved a bit cramped. "Why not move up into the third-floor attic?" suggested her parents. "The ceilings are a little low, but there is more floor space and even a private bath. It's just being used for storage."

The first night that Eleanor spent up in the attic was uneventful. But the second night, a window she had left open was closed when she awoke. On subsequent nights, doors and windows left closed were found open in the morning, or vice versa. Personal objects such as her hairbrush turned up in locations different from where she had left them.

All of this was unnerving enough, but then she began hearing mysterious footsteps where no person could have been. The unaccountable events seemed to escalate in frequency, inducing a growing feeling of fear in Eleanor.

Anxiety and uneasiness turned to terror one evening. Just after retiring for the night, Eleanor felt the bed sag as though another person had gotten into bed with her. An icy breath whispered in her ear, "Get out! Get out!"

She got out, moving back down to the smaller bedroom on the second floor. Once she was established back on the second floor, the ghostly harassment stopped.

When her parents asked the neighbors about the history of the old house, they were told that years before, the residents had included a mentally disabled, disfigured girl who had been confined to the third floor all her life. It seems that for that unfortunate girl, the attic was her entire world. Apparently, she had never really left in spirit, and her ghost resented and repelled any long-term intrusion into her territory.

When the attic again was used only for storage, the mysterious events and noises disappeared. The ghost made evident that she just wanted to be left alone.

Captain Huddy's Ghost

The ghost of Revolutionary War captain Joshua Huddy is one of the most famous, and frequently seen, phantoms of the Jersey Shore.

Captain Huddy, from a prominent Monmouth County family, was hanged from a tall tree atop the Highlands on April 12, 1782. Surely his last sight on earth was of Sandy Hook and its bay, where he had valiantly served his country, only to be foully murdered by his opponents, the occupying British Army.

Sandy Hook in those days was of great importance to both the Americans and the British. The Revolutionaries needed to watch British ship movements to and from New York City, which was occupied by the enemy. The British needed to protect Sandy Hook Lighthouse against the rebels, who were trying to destroy it in order to increase the chances of British shipwrecks. British naval squadrons frequently assembled in the shelter of Sandy Hook Bay and topped off their casks of fresh water at the "spout," a clear, cool spring at the foot of the Highlands, which had been visited by sailors since the days of Henry Hudson.

British forces had been out to get Huddy for some time, as he was a well-known patriot and able soldier who inspired great loyalty and courage in his men. Before they finally captured Huddy, they attacked him in his own home when spies reported that he was alone, as his men were out on patrol. Huddy's house was being used to store weapons, and when the British attacked, his African

American servant girl loaded and reloaded guns, which Huddy rapidly fired from different windows, fooling his attackers into thinking that many American soldiers were inside.

On a later occasion, while leading an attack on British troops stationed on Sandy Hook, Huddy was captured and taken to prison in chains. His captors, who were continually being harassed by American patrols and aware of being observed by spies, were lusting to find an excuse to make an example of a rebel. They accused Captain Huddy of having killed Philip White, a British soldier. It was a trumped-up charge, and the British knew it could not be true, as White had been shot after Captain Huddy was taken prisoner. But hang him they did, and in doing so they created a martyr to the American cause.

Before he was hanged, Huddy was given time to write out his will. When he mounted the scaffold, the captain was surprised to see that his execution was directed by his former friend and prewar neighbor Richard Lippincott, a loyalist who now held the rank of captain in the British Army.

The public on both sides of the Atlantic was outraged when the treachery and vindictiveness of the British commanders became known. But more than a martyr was created on that April day so long ago. The restless spirit of the wronged soldier still roams the bayshores, watching for British warships approaching and making sure that any people encountered on his nightly patrols are true and patriotic Americans.

It is said that many have seen a man clad in the uniform of a Revolutionary War officer wandering the shores of Sandy Hook. The apparition seems intent on approaching the observer, but at the last moment he turns away and mysteriously disappears. This disappearing act usually occurs just after the soldier has heard the voices of those he met. Was he listening for an English accent?

Woe to the Englishman that the officer meets on his lonely patrols, for many believe that the lonely figure is the ghost of Captain Joshua Huddy, who still prowls the beaches seeking vengeance on the British troops who hanged him for murder—a murder they knew he did not commit.

But this ghost story doesn't end here. By some accounts, Captain Huddy's ghost sometimes is seen in company with another ghost, said to be that of the British captain John Asgill. The two men appear to be discussing politics like old friends. Although they never met in life, it is fitting that their ghosts should talk, for Huddy and Asgill are connected in a strange way: Asgill was, at one time, slated to die in revenge for the cold-blooded murder of Huddy.

Captain Asgill had been held prisoner by American forces. Following Huddy's execution, he was chosen to die in protest of British treachery. Asgill's family back in England, however, was very well connected both politically and socially, and King George personally asked that Asgill's life be spared. Queen Marie Antoinette of France requested that the Count of Vergennes, French ambassador to the United States, ask Congress to call off Asgill's scheduled hanging. Congress, realizing that the war soon would be won anyway, passed a special law setting Asgill free if the British officially apologized, which they did. And today the ghosts of Huddy and Asgill are said to walk together on occasion, arguing military history and politics.

A Presidential Ghost

This particular ghost was seen most frequently in the closing decades of the nineteenth century, although a few sightings have been reported in recent years. Perhaps this spirit is no longer as restless as he once was, for his tragic death at Long Branch took place more than 125 years ago.

A tall, distinguished-looking gentleman strolls slowly along Ocean Avenue near the intersection with Lincoln Avenue. His receding hairline gives him the appearance of having a high, domed forehead. He has a mustache and full beard, in the high fashion of the Victorian era. His seaside walks appear to take place mostly in late evening during summer and early fall. The apparition seems to take no notice of anyone else, but if approached, the image dissolves in the salt air. Those who have seen the ghost believe it is that of James A. Garfield, twentieth president of the United States, who died on September 19, 1881.

Why would President Garfield's ghost still wander along the seashore at Long Branch? This was his favorite resort, and it was the place of his death following a long, painful struggle with the wounds he received from an assassin's bullet. Only a few months after his inauguration, Garfield was shot with a .44-caliber pistol while in Washington's train station. It was an abdominal wound, one that did not kill him right away. Unlike the massive head wounds that killed Presidents Lincoln and Kennedy, Garfield's wound would have been survivable if it had occurred in an age when antibiotics were available. As it was, the president lingered, in great pain but lucid, for seventy-eight days after being shot.

Most of those days were spent at Long Branch, in a cottage on the grounds of the old Elberon Hotel, long since demolished. The White House had been judged inappropriate for Garfield's feverish convalescence, as Washington was notoriously hot and humid, a miserable climate in the days before air-conditioning. Garfield had enjoyed the cool ocean breezes at Long Branch on vacations, so why not try to recover at the Jersey shore?

But Garfield's agonizingly slow death could not be averted by salt air. His death most likely resulted from the doctors' continual probing for the bullet with unclean fingers and nonsterile instruments. Many Civil War veterans were walking around with bullets still in them, but Garfield's doctors were determined to remove it. The ailing president finally died from massive infection, as he gazed out the window of his seafront cottage by the ocean he had always loved to visit—and perhaps still visits long after his death.

The End of an Era

So near and yet so far. That must have been among the last thoughts of many immigrants as the ship that had brought them to the very shores of the New World was wrecked in plain view of safety.

In 1854, about four hundred eager immigrants set sail on the *New Era*, a ship that was supposed to carry them from Europe to their new homes in America. They traveled safely across the Atlantic Ocean but, with the town of Asbury Park in sight, became the victims of a sudden rough storm. The ship, swamped by icy waves and brutal winds, was abruptly grounded off the coast. Rescue workers labored to bring as many passengers as possible to shore, using the newly invented life-car system, which reached the ship on a cable, but the *New Era* sank with almost two-thirds of the passengers still on board. When the weather cleared and rescue workers were able to board the ship, they soon discovered a sad truth: Many of the immigrants had turned their small savings into gold and silver coins, which they had sewn into the lining of their clothes. This small amount of money, which would have been barely enough to help them start life over in a new land, had been sufficient to weigh them down and keep them from surfacing in the ship's hold, resulting in their untimely death. Their ghosts are said to wander along the beaches at night, jingling the coins that had kept them from swimming to safety.

That same year, the packet *Powhatan* went aground off the coast of Brigantine, sheared in two by a violent storm. Local residents brought about forty bodies to shore and buried them at Rum Point, but many others were seen floating in the bay. Two brothers, Isaac and Robert Smith of Smithville, reportedly retrieved as many of the passengers as they could and buried them in a common grave in the old Quaker cemetery in their town. Travelers through the area have reported that a swirling, white mist is periodically seen drifting around the cemetery, especially after a storm.

The Ghost in the Library

Monmouth University is located in West Long Branch, a clam-shell's throw from the beach. West Long Branch once was home to the superrich, and one of its old mansions may still house a famous ghost.

The fabulously wealthy Guggenheim family built a summer home there, modeled on Versailles' Petite Trianon Palace. This beautiful mansion now houses Monmouth University's library, which is haunted. Every night at midnight, a lovely phantom, exquisitely gowned and bedecked with diamonds, slowly descends the grand staircase. At the bottom of the steps, she vanishes.

There are two different identifications of this beautiful specter. She is said to be the ghost of either Mrs. Benjamin Guggenheim or her daughter-in-law Leone, Mrs. Murray Guggenheim.

Benjamin Guggenheim was one of the world's wealthiest men when he died on the evening of April 15, 1912. The son of a poor immigrant who began his career selling shoelaces from a pushcart, Benjamin inherited a $100 million fortune based on mining and smelting metals. He became famous for his bravery and gallantry one tragic night on the North Atlantic when he refused a place on a lifeboat leaving a sinking liner. He stepped aside, saying, "No woman will be left aboard this ship because Ben Guggenheim is a

coward." His own wife was at home in West Long Branch as Ben went down with the ship—the *Titanic*. Is it his widow or his daughter-in-law that still walks down the stairs, perhaps remembering Ben's heroic gesture that cost him his life?

The Spy House and Its Many Ghosts

While many old houses are said to be haunted by a ghost or two, one old house in Port Monmouth is alleged to contain at least thirty. The Whitlock-Seabrook House, dating to 1663, probably is the oldest house on the Jersey coast. It is also known as the Spy House, because American spies used to frequent the area to watch for British ships entering or leaving New York Harbor. After a hard day's work of espionage, these agents would drop by the Whitlock-Seabrook House, used as a tavern at the time, for a few drinks and an exchange of information.

The famous old structure now houses the Shoal Harbor Museum, part of Monmouth County's Bayshore waterfront park. It is open to the public, who may or may not see any of the thirty-some ghosts in residence.

One of the Spy House's more famous ghosts is said to inhabit an old mannequin called Abigail, named for a young girl who once occupied an upper room. The real-life Abigail grew up in the house, married, and bore four children, all of whom died in infancy. Abigail the dummy is said to cry on occasion, accompanied by the sounds of wailing infants. Another resident ghost, that of a boy, likes to tap visitors on their shoulders. When they turn around, they see nothing. Several of the Spy House's ghosts spend much of their time lurking in the shrubbery outside, still spying on ships out in the bay.

The county park administrators in charge of the house prefer to downplay the ghost stories, as they are concerned that the house's true historical significance could get lost in the notoriety of the ghosts. But as some of these ghosts have hung around for three centuries, they'll probably outlast the bureaucratic nonbelievers.

The Lady Who Didn't Want to Leave

The majestic old Essex and Sussex Hotel, now a condo, dominates the skyline at Spring Lake. The huge structure, with its distinctive domed towers, overlooks both the ocean and lake. Many visitors to Spring Lake, seeing the grand old hotel for the first time, have a feeling they've somehow seen it before. They have, if they've seen the 1981 James Cagney film *Ragtime*, which had some scenes filmed at the Essex and Sussex.

The gracious old hotel has a gracious old ghost, or so some believe. A local tradition is that a longtime resident of the hotel, an elderly, wealthy woman whom we will call Alice, so loved the place she'd called home for decades that she never left, at least in spirit. In life, Alice was a "night person" who loved to sleep late and stay up to enjoy the sedately sophisticated entertainment and conversation in the hotel's lounge bar. And so, late every evening, Alice's spirit makes her grand entrance down the elegant staircase. Beautifully dressed and immaculately groomed, the smiling matron is heading for her customary nightcap in the familiar setting of the quietly elegant bar. Life was just so good at the Essex and Sussex that she couldn't bear to leave.

Alice never disturbs anyone. When observers look again at the staircase, she is gone, leaving people to doubt whether they ever really saw her at all.

The Devil and the Drunkard

They tell an old story around the fishing port of Belmar and neighboring seashore towns about the man who was told to stop drinking by the Devil himself. One Jack Slocum was well known in a little tavern by the Shark River. Slocum was a drunk. He just did not know when to stop. In the early nineteenth century, per capita liquor consumption was much higher than it is today, and Slocum's drinking was notable even back then. He drank so much every night that it became the habit of the bartender, with the help of some of Slocum's drinking buddies, to heave the semiconscious man up into his wagon and let the horse find its own way home. In those days, the horse was a kind of designated driver as it headed for the barn without direction from its owner.

One night, as the story goes, Slocum's horse and wagon were stopped by a tall, well-dressed man on the road home. The sight of this man, who was ordinary looking except for his glowing red eyes, was enough to instantly sober Slocum. "If you don't stop drinking," the Devil told him, "I'll take your soul in one year's time!"

Slocum believed this satanic warning. To the amazement of all, he stopped drinking. Not a drop passed his lips. He missed his drinking bouts. He even missed the hangovers. He counted the days, looking forward to that first glorious drink. After 365 days of stone-cold sobriety, Slocum figured he'd stayed alcohol-free for a year and, in so doing, had put himself beyond the Devil's reach. Party time! Jack Slocum had his drink, and then a lot more. When he passed out, the bartender and Slocum's drinking buddies dutifully put him in his wagon, propped up on the driver's seat, and sent the horse on its way home.

But Slocum never made it. It was discovered the next day that his wagon had run off the road and into the Shark River. The horse had escaped, but poor Slocum was tangled in the reins and drowned. Had the Devil cheated on his threat to Slocum not to drink for a year or else? No, it was Slocum who hadn't paid close enough attention to the calendar—it was a leap year, one of 366 days in length.

The Lost Explorer

Sandy Hook seems to host a rather large population of ghosts, some famous, some not so famous. The oldest non-Indian ghost in New Jersey haunts Sandy Hook—that of an explorer who got left behind in a new and, for him, dangerous world.

In September 1609, the famed adventurer Henry Hudson was exploring along the Jersey coast. He was just about to sail north into history, for ahead of him was a voyage up the magnificent river that now bears his name. Hudson was a freelance explorer, and although he and most of his crew aboard the *Half Moon* were English, he was currently working for the Dutch. Whatever land he claimed to have discovered would belong to them.

Maybe that explains why Hudson did not bother to get off his ship when it anchored in Sandy Hook Bay. His first officer, Robert Juet, recorded in his diary that Raritan Bay and the Navesink Highlands, the highest point on the coast south of Maine, was "a very good land to fall with [come to from the sea] and a pleasant land to see." But Hudson decided to stay on board, assigning others to get into the rowboats and explore more closely—a wise move on Hudson's part.

Hudson's men in their rowboats encountered a band of Indians in their canoes. The Europeans generally were favorably impressed by the local Indians and thought them to be handsome and robust ("well made," in the language of the day). They initially believed that the natives were friendly, but on this occasion, they were not so welcoming. Someone must have been having a bad day. There is no record of which side started it, but guns were fired at the Indians, who responded with a blizzard of arrows.

No one knows how many Indians may have been killed, but only one Englishman, John Coleman, died in the exchange. His comrades buried poor John on Sandy Hook, in an unmarked grave to deter the Indians from digging him up and desecrating his body.

And so the ghost of the first English casualty in what became the European invasion of New Jersey walks along the beach, looking out to sea, trying to spot the *Half Moon.* Coleman's is a lonely vigil, for the *Half Moon* never returned to Sandy Hook. His is a nonthreatening ghost that, if approached, simply disappears.

Penelope's Nightmare Honeymoon

One of the few female ghosts that frequent Sandy Hook is that of Penelope Van Princis Stout. Occasionally sighted near the tip of Sandy Hook, the ghost appears to be looking about anxiously for help. And in her life's sojourn on Sandy Hook, Penelope needed a lot of help. Poor Penelope survived what must be one of the most nightmarish of honeymoons.

Penelope was a newlywed when she and her husband boarded a Dutch ship to take them to a new life in the New World. They were heading for the Dutch colony of New Amsterdam and had almost made it there when a violent storm wrecked their ship on the shores of Sandy Hook in 1640. Most of the crew and passengers managed to swim ashore. Since Sandy Hook provided little in the way of food sources and was then a wild and isolated place, most shipwreck survivors decided to start walking until they found some Dutch settlement.

But the Van Princises stayed behind. Penelope chose to stay with her husband, who was very sick, and nurse him back to health. Despite having only wild beach plums and clams to eat, Penelope had begun to restore her husband's vitality when a band of hostile Indians appeared. They killed her helpless husband, leaving Penelope for dead with a fractured skull, crippled left arm, and severe gashes on her stomach.

Against the odds, Penelope somehow survived all this and wandered Sandy Hook desperately looking for help. Her cries and arm-waving didn't come to the notice of ships bound to or from New Amsterdam. But she persisted. Finally, a few Indians found her and took pity on the gallant survivor, half dead from her wounds. They nursed her back to health and then helped her reach New Amsterdam.

The story has a happy ending. Penelope got married again, to a former British sailor, Richard Stout, and lived the rest of her life at Middletown, only about five miles from where she had spent her nightmarish introduction to life in the New World. Still, her ghost seems to be drawn to Sandy Hook, where once she paced the beach forlornly crying for help. If you see her spirit anxiously looking for assistance, just reassure her that help is on the way and that she would eventually die in bed, surrounded by her ten children, seventy-two years after her nightmare honeymoon.

The Ghostly Noah's Ark

Fishermen and pleasure boaters off the shores of Sandy Hook occasionally report fleeting glimpses of an American version of Noah's Ark. The antique sailing vessel appears to be carrying a variety of animals on deck: cattle, sheep, and crates of poultry. The phantom ship most likely is the bold spirit of a classic example of American ingenuity and craftiness versus British power and guns.

During the War of 1812, ships of the British Navy, then the mightiest in the world, cruised off New Jersey's coast. Far from their home base, the British sailors frequently needed to reprovision their food supplies, and they did not hesitate to steal food from American farms and ships. They had a habit of landing along the shores of New Jersey's bays and rivers and helping themselves to livestock. The British especially enjoyed a free roast beef dinner at the expense of helpless American farmers. The Americans finally decided to lure a British warship into a trap baited with cattle, sheep, and poultry.

The ship *Yankee* was disguised as a livestock carrier, but belowdecks she carried determined American marines. The *Yankee* deliberately sailed close to the British sloop *Eagle*, then on patrol off Sandy Hook to catch American merchant ships. The *Eagle*, tempted by the livestock on view on the *Yankee*'s deck, ordered the American to heave to and prepare for boarding. As the *Eagle* came alongside, the *Yankee*'s marines leaped onto the British ship, firing their guns. The *Yankee* had turned the tables, and the "helpless livestock carrier" instead took the *Eagle* as a prize and sailed her into New York. It was July 4, 1813, and a fireworks display greeted the captured *Eagle*. It was reported that the victorious Americans all enjoyed a huge barbecue of the "bait."

The Wrestling Match on the Beach

Up in Long Branch, old-timers still tell the story of the ghostly wrestlers on the beach. It is a tale that goes back to the early Colonial period, one that involved trickery on both sides. The ghost wrestlers are an Indian brave and an Englishman named John Slocum. It was a serious match, with a great deal of land and money at stake on the outcome.

The year was 1688. English colonists already were established at Middletown and Shrewsbury, and they wanted to purchase land between those settlements and the ocean. They contacted the local Indians with an offer to negotiate.

Now it happened that a favorite sport among the Indians was wrestling. A good wrestling match always drew gambling on the outcome. The local tribe currently had a champion wrestler living among them, a man named Vow-A-Vapon, who was not only powerful, but very tricky as well. In the Indian wrestling tradition, anything goes. The only rule was that there were no rules.

To discuss the terms of a land deal, the Indians invited their English neighbors to a clambake on the beach at what is now Long Branch. The entertainment would be a wrestling match. How much land did the whites care to purchase? What would be the price? The Indians suggested that the wrestling match would resolve these questions. The winner would set the terms.

The Indian's secret weapon was the unbeaten Vow-A-Vapon. The English chose John Slocum to represent them. As the match was to begin, the Indian champion smeared himself with a thick layer of bear grease. Slocum's side protested this as unfair. The Indians replied that in their tradition, it was not breaking any rules. Slocum couldn't get ahold of his slippery opponent—until, that is, he threw handfuls of beach sand on the greasy Indian to increase the friction of his grip. The evenly matched athletes wrestled for two grueling hours before Slocum finally won. "Slocum's Purchase" ran from the ocean back to what is now Eatontown. And on occasion, the ghosts of the two wrestlers still grapple on the beach at Long Branch. Stay well clear of them—one of them throws sand.

The Captain and the Pigeon

Visitors to the very tip of Sandy Hook report seeing a ghostly man chasing after an equally ghostly pigeon. The man never quite catches the bird, which flutters and struts just out of reach. An ornery bird and a frustrated man—their spirits are forever linked in a contest between them that dates to the early 1850s.

Man and bird both were made famous in an article in *Scribner's Magazine* more than 150 years ago. It seems that both the man, one Captain Farrell, and the carrier pigeon, called Dickie, were key employees of the Western Union Telegraph Company, which operated a system of transmitting messages from ships approaching New York Harbor to shipping companies in Manhattan. Half a century before Marconi perfected the wireless telegraph and half a dozen years before the transatlantic cable was laid, incoming ships could not give advance notice of their approach to their cargo owners, arrange dock space, contact warehouses, or do other business until they docked. At least, not without Dickie and Captain Farrell.

Western Union maintained a seventy-foot-high wooden tower at Sandy Hook, which was Dickie's home base. As a ship entered the channel past Sandy Hook, a small boat would carry Dickie out to the ship, where a message would be attached to the bird's leg. Dickie would fly home, where the captain would retrieve the message and then telegraph the information to New York.

Dickie, however, had a very independent, not to say sadistic, streak in his bird brain. He made a game of staying just out of Captain Farrell's reach at first. Dickie enjoyed being coaxed. The bird would always come to the captain, but not before making the captain beg. Dickie never got lost flying back home and was a fast flier, and the company had high regards for the bird. The captain, however, may have wanted to put Dickie in a casserole. When the transatlantic cable made it possible for shipping companies to report the dispatch of cargo ships as they left port in 1858, Dickie and the captain were retired. Maybe Dickie ended up on the captain's dinner plate after all.

But their spirits live on, dueling across the sands in a continuing contest of ornery bird and angry man.

The Indian Who Refused to Go Along

People near Eatontown, a few miles inland from Long Branch, report seeing a phantom figure strolling along the backroads late at night, carrying a large, bloody tomahawk. Supposedly this is the ghost of Indian Will, a loner who may have been psychotic.

It seems that Indian Will was a very independent-minded member of the Lenni-Lenape tribe. He kept to himself, did not socialize with either Indians or whites, and was thought to beat his wife, his only companion. He definitely did not honor the tribe's collective decisions.

In 1762, the first Indian reservation in the country was created by the colony of New Jersey. A 3,284-acre tract of land in Burlington County was set aside for the state's first people. It was to be tax-free, and the Lenni-Lenape were encouraged to settle there and adopt a European lifestyle. The community, known as Brotherton (now Indian Mills), was equipped with European-style houses, a store, a meetinghouse, and a gristmill.

But Indian Will refused to join the rest of his tribe at Brotherton. He wanted nothing to do with becoming an "imitation white man," as he put it. The tribal leaders, fearing that Indian Will's refusal to move away from his ancestral home near the seashore would jeopardize their agreement with the government of New Jersey, tried to get him to go along with the tribe's decision. They sent a messenger to see him, but the messenger never returned. Another messenger was sent, but he disappeared as well.

Indian Will had killed them with his tomahawk. And when his wife expressed a desire to join the others at Brotherton, he drowned her. Indian Will never left home, either in body or spirit. He and his bloody tomahawk can still be seen on moonless nights, wandering the familiar roads of home.

Incidentally, in a way, Indian Will was right about not wanting to go to Brotherton. The experimental community failed and was abandoned by the Lenni-Lenape in 1801, when the last sixty-three inhabitants of the reservation moved to New York State to join other Indians. But the Indian who wouldn't go along with his tribe remains on his ancestral land, if only as a ghost.

Molly Still Brings the Pitcher

A family vacationing at the Jersey Shore recently decided to take a side trip, only ten or twelve miles from Long Branch, to visit Monmouth Battlefield State Park, where one of the more famous battles of the Revolution had been fought. It was a brutally hot and humid day, the kind of weather that sends tens of thousands to New Jersey's beaches. The visitors were charmed to find a tour guide, appropriately dressed in Colonial costume, playing the role of Molly Pitcher and offering them cool water from the famous Revolutionary War figure's well.

"Molly Pitcher" was a real person, born Mary Ludwig in Carlisle, Pennsylvania. Her place in American history was earned on June 28, 1778, when she accompanied her husband, Private William Hays, on the battlefield at Monmouth as the Revolutionary War battle began. It was a blisteringly hot day, and Mary, nicknamed Molly, began bringing pitchers of water to her husband and his comrades. Private Hays served as a gunner in the 1st Pennsylvania Artillery, and tending one of the big iron guns was hot work. The 96-degree heat was almost as terrible as the bullets flying between the two armies. Thirty-seven Americans and fifty-nine British soldiers died of sunstroke in their woolen uniforms. "Molly, bring the pitcher!" was a frequent cry among the exhausted soldiers, a plea that soon was shortened to "Molly Pitcher!"

Not only did the men desperately need cool water, but the cannons themselves needed to be sponged off to remove old gunpowder residue and cool the hot metal.

When Molly's husband fell wounded and a comrade was killed by enemy fire, Molly took her husband's place at the gun and kept firing. After the battle, Molly was thanked in person by General Nathanael Greene. He later presented her to General George Washington, who made her an honorary officer on the spot. Molly remained with the Army for eight years and was given a half-pay pension when she retired. Her husband recovered from his wound, and now outranked by his officer wife, they lived on into old age together. Molly was buried with full military honors.

When the tourist family went on from Molly Pitcher's well to the Monmouth County Historical Museum, they complimented the staff there on the costumed guide impersonating Molly Pitcher. "But there is no one dressed as Molly Pitcher at the well," they were assured. No one. Drink up.

Central Shore

The Hoodoo Schooner

Some ships, like some people, seem to be just plain unlucky. If there's trouble to be had, they manage to find it. Sailors call a perennially unlucky ship a "hoodoo," a word that appears to be connected to the ancient superstitions of African-Caribbean voodoo.

Such a ship was the steel-hulled schooner *Nathaniel Palmer*, which seemed to be dogged by bad luck. In her first major brush with disaster, she ran aground on Long Beach during a storm on March 17, 1901. She sat on the beach like a dead whale until she finally was towed off, her hull still intact but her masts and rigging a shambles. All her crew were rescued.

Reoutfitted, she sailed the coastal waters again, but the schooner seemed to travel in a perpetual fog of mishap. Cargo would somehow fall overboard, sails would blow away in a storm, and her sailors frequently had nightmares of falling overboard and drowning. Still, the *Nathaniel Palmer* sailed on, always struggling back to port with all her crew safe.

On her most unlucky day, during World War I, the schooner was torpedoed off Cape May by a German submarine. Why the sub attacked the inoffensive old sailing ship instead of going after bigger game remains a mystery. The *Nathaniel Palmer* went to the bottom quickly, but again her crew all were saved. One second thought, maybe the hoodoo ship actually was a lucky ship, in that no one ever lost his life sailing on her. Some sailors claim that in bad storms, one can catch a glimpse of the ghost of the *Nathaniel Palmer* still sailing into the wind, unlucky as ever.

Still Following the North Star

Four horses strain to pull the heavy freight wagon down backwoods roads toward the little port of Toms River—and toward freedom, for the phantom wagon carries spirits from the Underground Railroad. The Underground Railroad was not a railroad at all, although trains were occasionally used, along with boats, wagons, and carriages. It was an organized system of moving runaway slaves in secret, and thus "underground." Toms River was an important station on the pathway to freedom—so important in American history, and in human triumphs and tragedies, that the ghosts of long-ago "passengers" repeatedly travel through the area.

New Jersey's geography and history made it a vital link in the Underground Railroad. Runaway slaves followed the North Star, moving secretively by night. The most heavily used routes came north along Chesapeake and Delaware Bays. Sympathetic northerners then helped the runaways cross New Jersey to reach ships at Perth Amboy, Jersey City, or Toms River. The sleepy little port of Toms River offered less chance of detection or interference than the others. The goal was to reach Canada, where no American authorities could recapture the runaways.

Whites and free blacks working as guides, or "conductors," on the Underground Railroad were putting their own freedom on the line, as the infamous Fugitive Slave Act made it a criminal offense to assist the runaways in any fashion. And so the "conductors" and their "passengers" traveled by night, silently, following the North Star, which pointed to freedom.

A prominent organizer of this underground railroad was William Still, the twenty-first and youngest child of parents who themselves had fled slavery in Maryland. Still devoted his life to helping slaves escape and was especially active in organizing the Philadelphia-Mount Holly-Toms River route. His tall, distinguished form is prominent among the ghosts moving quietly along backroads toward the ships that waited at Toms River so long ago.

Should you witness the ghostly caravan some dark night, wish it well silently.

Bringing Home the Bacon

On the shores of Little Egg Harbor, near the old village of West Creek, people have spotted not just one ghost, but a ghostly mob. The group of angry spirits seems to be chasing, catching, and then beating and shooting to death a tall figure in their midst. Are the phantoms reenacting a famous incident from the American Revolution?

John Bacon was the leader of a notorious band of thugs who practiced piracy, murder, theft, and general mayhem from their wartime hangout on what is now Island Beach State Park. Bacon and his crew claimed that they were loyalists, supporting King George's cause against his rebellious subjects. More likely, though, Bacon's true loyalties were to himself and his criminal gang, and he simply used the skirmishes between loyalists and patriots as cover for his murderous greed.

Bacon and his men carried out the infamous Long Beach massacre in the fall of 1782. An English ship, grounded on Barnegat Shoals near the present lighthouse, was abandoned. The ship was then found by the American privateer *Alligator*, captained by a Captain Steelman of Cape May. Steelman and his men salvaged the cargo of tea, intending to sell it in Tuckerton.

Bacon's gang crept up on the men as they slept that night, exhausted from the work of unloading and transporting the salvaged cargo onto the beach, and murdered Steelman and six others. A posse of patriots hunted down the culprits, promising to "bring home the bacon," and they finally did. They caught up to Bacon at West Creek. It is said that Bacon's severed head was displayed at a local tavern for years afterward in revenge for the Long Beach massacre.

Parental Love Never Dies

It happens every winter in the little resort town of Barnegat Light. One or both parents are taking their baby out in a carriage or stroller for some fresh air on a sunny day. Near the seafront, they encounter a handsome couple in oddly out-of-date clothing. The man is resplendent in a dark blue naval uniform with well-polished brass buttons, his wife in a fur-trimmed coat, scarf, and elaborate hat, dressed for a chilly if bright day. Smiling, the strange couple approach the baby carriage, "What a lovely baby!" they exclaim. "A truly beautiful child. You must take very good care of it." "But," one will say to the other, "it is not ours."

Suddenly they are gone, having seemingly evaporated like a wisp of morning mist as the warming sun rises. Belatedly, the local couple taking their baby for a little outing realize that they have just seen the famous ghosts of Barnegat. Encounters with phantoms can be a little unsettling, even when, as in this case, the spirits are friendly and well-meaning.

The story begins in the late nineteenth century, when a coastal schooner ran aground in a January storm. The Coast Guard, as was customary in those days, used a specially designed gun to fire a grappling hook attached to a cable out to the stranded vessel. A large, torpedo-shaped life car was then sent out on the cable, and one by one, the sailors entered the enclosed iron container and were pulled safely ashore. The ship's owner and captain, however, chose to stay behind, knowing that an abandoned ship could be claimed for salvage and he would lose his investment. His wife and baby daughter also were aboard. The wife decided to stay with her husband, as the schooner had an iron hull and seemed in no danger of breaking up in the heavy surf. But they sent their child to safety in the arms of the first mate.

The ship survived the night intact, but the captain and his wife died of exposure in the bitterly cold winds that lashed the vessel. Ever since, the ghostly pair stroll the little town, looking for their baby girl in every carriage they spot. They are harmless in their eternal quest to once again hold their baby safely in their arms.

The Jersey Shore's Most Famous Ghost

The story of the Woman in White may be the single most often repeated ghost saga set along New Jersey's seashore. Why are some ghosts, such as this one, so frequently featured in local folklore, while other tales of the supernatural remain obscure? Perhaps for the same reason that a certain few fairy tales, out of many in traditional folk literature, always make the top-ten lists. A good story offers a moral, a great truth in which people believe, and one they are compelled to pass on to the next generation.

The various versions of the Woman in White story certainly have a moral. Set on Long Beach Island, they describe a local woman, the daughter of a family of wreckers—people who deliberately caused shipwrecks in order to loot the cargoes—who falls in love with a young, ambitious sailor. The two wish to wed. The sailor plans one more long journey, which will take months to complete, in order to save enough money for a honeymoon and a cottage. The couple plan to marry on his return.

Days after his departure, the young woman participates in a wrecking operation. After the victimized ship runs aground and is pounded by the surf, she wanders along the beach, looking for corpses to strip of their money and jewelry. Alas, she comes across the dead body of her lover. He just couldn't wait to reunite with her, so he had jumped ship and taken a vessel heading back home early.

In some versions, the ghost of the Woman in White (wearing her wedding gown, of course) still wanders the beaches looking for her lover. One story has her digging a grave on the beach in which to bury her sailor, led to his untimely doom by her own greed and treachery. In this story, the woman's frantic digging, always late at night, is an endless, frustrating chore as the loose sand keeps sliding back into the hole. Weeping, the ghost keeps on digging, paying penance for her sins.

The moral? It is the universal truth that the evil that one does can come back at one like a boomerang. Stay well clear of the phantom nighttime grave digger on Long Beach Island.

Help! Shark!

One popular theory is that ghosts frequently result from sudden, untimely, and violent deaths—deaths that leave the victim's spirit disoriented, trapped between two worlds. Are these pathetic spirits doomed to relive, over and over, their last agonizing moments among the living?

Such seems to be the case of the ghost of a shark victim at Beach Haven. This death occurred in July 1916. A wealthy young bachelor from Philadelphia had escaped the heat for the trendy new resort of Beach Haven. Young and athletic, he decided on a solitary, late-afternoon swim. His is a well-documented story, as he was the first victim in a horrific series of fatal shark attacks that summer.

Late on summer afternoons to this day, visitors to Beach Haven sometimes witness a bather in distress.

"Help! Shark!" He screams as a triangular black fin slices the water.

Those brave enough to approach, however, find nothing but a swirl of red in the water. The flood of color quickly disperses.

Did they see an actual shark attack, or only the phantom image of a long-ago tragedy?

Shark experts claim that the young vacationer made two big mistakes in venturing into the water. He was wearing a then fashionable black bathing suit that covered him from his thighs to his chest. He was accompanied into the water by a large black dog. And he may have assumed, mistakenly, that large sharks are denizens of tropical waters, not places like the Jersey shore. Actually, many species of sharks known to attack people—blues, hammerheads, makos, and great whites—cruise in New Jersey coastal waters.

It is claimed that sharks don't find people as satisfying a meal as seals, which have a very high fat content, and attack humans only out of confusion. A black bathing suit could have led a shark to think it was pursuing a big, tasty seal. Also, the irregular thrashing about of a swimming dog mimics the splashing of a fish in distress—catnip to a cruising shark.

Looking for Pirates' Trees

A common theme in many stories of buried treasure is the "pirate's tree." Long before global positioning technology, or even reasonably accurate maps, pirates had a problem with buried treasure. How would they ever find it again? The empty beaches, which were favorite places for burying treasure, had few landmarks. The story is that pirates liked to bury their treasure chests near unusually large trees, which then became the markers to guide the treasure hunters in retrieving their loot.

The notorious pirate Blackbeard is alleged to have had a habit of burying a luckless companion atop the treasure chest, whose ghost would then guard the treasure. At least on some occasions, Blackbeard would ask for volunteer victims. He would reassure the man to be left on guard for eternity that he would use a "charmed" bullet, one that would kill, but would allow the ghost to rise up and protect the treasure until the rightful owners returned. After the charmed bullet was fired into the pirate's heart, he would be buried in an upright position, waiting to spring into action if looters appeared. In some versions of the story, a large, vicious black dog also was shot with a charmed bullet so the animal's ghost could help defend the treasure.

On September 11, 1886, two men posing as surveyors called at the local Coast Guard station at Beach Haven to ask directions. Was there a large oak tree on the beach about two miles south of Beach Haven? When told that the dead skeleton of a large oak could still be seen near the inlet, the men left. Curious, the Coast Guard men visited the area the next day and found that a large hole had been dug. Some rotten wood was found, along with a rusty, gold-hilted sword. Whatever else had been buried was gone. Did the two "surveyors" have an old treasure map? And did they run into a ghostly pirate and his canine companion?

The Lighthouse Builder's Ghost

This particular ghost has not been seen for some time. Perhaps the general's spirit has moved on to some other earthly—or unearthly—haunt. The seldom-seen ghost that used to walk around the narrow catwalk at the top of Barnegat Light is said to have been the spirit of George Gordon Meade, the hero of the Battle of Gettysburg. Meade was the designer and builder of the famous old lighthouse, which was finished in 1858, just a few years before the outbreak of the Civil War.

But if that was Meade's ghost atop Barnegat Light, why would his spirit be attracted to this lighthouse instead of the scene of his greatest military triumph, Gettysburg? Perhaps his spirit's appearance at Barnegat Lighthouse rather than on the bloody battlefields of Gettysburg says something about his character. While the great victory at Gettysburg, a turning point in the Civil War, ensured the survival of the Union and brought justifiable fame to Meade, he must have been awed and horrified by the number of deaths in what was the largest battle, in terms of total casualties, ever fought on the continent.

Building the 172-foot-high lighthouse at Barnegat Inlet was a triumph of engineering, and George Meade's West Point education had made him a professional engineer. Here was a well-designed, solidly constructed contribution to the nation's welfare and maritime safety. It was unblemished by the spilled blood of scores of thousands of brave troops on both sides at Gettysburg. It was a happier, if less famous, accomplishment.

As his Civil War record proved, Meade was a resourceful planner, determined to learn from others' mistakes. His enduring, sturdy lighthouse still stands sentinel on the Jersey coast because, learning from the collapse of an earlier one on this spot, Meade anticipated and built it to withstand any possible attack by Mother Nature. His lighthouse has double brick walls ten feet thick at the base, with an air space between to prevent rot. Maybe his ghostly visits were an occasion to express his pride and satisfaction at his remarkable peacetime work. Well done, General. Rest in peace.

The Lighthouse Keeper's Ghost

There is another story about Barnegat Light that seldom shows up in official guidebooks. It is the story of the lighthouse keeper's ghost.

The present lighthouse, built by General Meade, is the second at that site. The first Barnegat Light, only forty feet tall, was built in 1834; it toppled into the waves on November 2, 1856, after the waves and currents eroded away three hundred feet of beach in front of it. Some old-timers believed that the present light sits atop the foundations of the first, and that a long-forgotten cellar room lies under the floor. The story goes that workmen repairing this floor once broke through into the cellar room unexpectedly. There, in the dank cellar, a skeleton sat in a rocking chair in front of a brick fireplace. In his lap was the skeleton of a cat, and clutched in the skull's mouth was an old brier pipe. Some believe that this skeleton was that of the light's first keeper, "Uncle Caleb" Parker. Uncle Caleb had sworn he'd never leave the light unattended. Perhaps he is still on duty. A few locals swear that on stormy winter nights, the smell of an old pipe filled with aromatic tobacco can be detected at the base of the light. Is Uncle Caleb still enjoying a pipe in front of his fireplace?

Uncle Caleb is famous locally for starting the tradition of the lucky cats of Barnegat. Barnegat Shoals earned its lighthouse because it was an incredibly dangerous part of the Jersey coast. In just a forty-year period, from 1838 to 1878, more than 125 ships were wrecked along a twenty-four-mile stretch of shoreline. One terrible night, it is said, a schooner went down within sight of the light, despite Uncle Caleb's best efforts. All souls were lost that night, but in the morning, the keeper spotted a cat clinging to debris just offshore. He rowed out in the dangerous surf to rescue the poor, frightened creature. This only survivor was a curious-looking cat, with no tail. It had short front legs and long back legs, so that its gait was more like a rabbit's than a cat's. No one could remember having seen such a cat before. It was a manx, a breed originating in the Isle of Man between Ireland and Britain. To Uncle Caleb, it was a very lucky cat to have survived a shipwreck.

This lucky cat, it turned out, was pregnant, and soon Uncle Caleb had a family of tailless cats. His neighbors were quite happy to take a kitten, as they believed that the tailless cats of Barnegat would bring good luck to any house. It is said that to this day, there are many manx cats in the neighborhood of Barnegat.

The Ghost of the Airship

For many years now, New Jerseyans living in Ocean County's coastal area, in a huge triangle formed between Point Pleasant Beach, Barnegat Inlet, and the Naval Air Engineering Center at

Lakehurst, have reported seeing an eerie shadow overhead. The unexplained experience generally happens like this: It is a day in spring, April or May. The day has started out fine and sunny, but the warm, rising air currents have produced towering thunderclouds. Thunderstorms, with their brief heavy rains accompanied by lightning and strong winds, especially turbulent in the cloud itself, are common occurrences everywhere in the warmer months. But in the Lakehurst Triangle, these storms in spring can be foreshadowed by a mysterious, elongated shadow passing overhead. It is as though a giant cigar or torpedo briefly blots out the sun. When the observer looks skyward, however, seeking the cause of this shadow, there is nothing but sky to see. Have these people seen the shadow of a ghost airship?

Lakehurst Naval Air Station has gone down in history as the site of one of the most famous air disasters: the explosion of the German airship Hindenburg. Thanks largely to dramatic pictures filmed by a newsreel crew present, this May 6, 1937, event is generally agreed to have marked the end of the era of the lighter-than-air dirigibles, or zeppelins, named after their German developer, Count von Zeppelin.

Invented in World War I for military purposes, these airships captured public attention because of their size and potential as passenger carriers. These giants were, at one time, serious rivals of heavier-than-air airplanes. The rigid-frame dirigibles (as compared with frameless balloons or blimps) could cruise for thousands of miles, at a time when airplanes cruising ranges were much shorter.

For a brief time, Lakehurst was an international air terminal. The German airship Graf Zeppelin began and ended its epic around-the-world trip here in 1929. Unlike the American airships, which were operated by the U.S. Navy for military reconnaissance, the German ones served as luxury civilian passenger carriers. And luxury is the word. With a capacity for only sixty-eight passengers, the Hindenburg was equipped with a dining room, library, observation lounge with grand piano, and no less than three bars.

The fiery end of the Hindenburg as she prepared to land at Lakehurst was such a widely publicized disaster that those witnessing the ghost shadow of a huge airship in the vicinity assume they have encountered the spirit of this tragic dirigible. Few remember, however, that several of the period's other airships also were wrecked.

The huge airships, even when filled with nonflammable helium instead of explosive hydrogen, as the Germans used, were fatally vulnerable to the violent wind shifts associated with thunderstorms. Although the much more famous Hindenburg explosion killed thirty-six people, seventy-three lives were lost when the U.S. Navy's airship Akron crashed into the sea off Barnegat Light on April 3, 1933.

And so, if the mysterious airship-size shadows that many claim to have seen in the Lakehurst Triangle are the ghosts of a doomed dirigible, is it the Hindenburg or Akron that still haunts the skies along the New Jersey coast? Or could it be both?

Though many have seen the mysterious shadow, a few claim to have seen the ghostly airship itself, still searching for a safe landing. The two airships' ghosts should be easy to identify. The Hindenburg was marked by giant Nazi swastikas on its stabilizing fins, whereas the Akron proudly carried the star-in-circle of the U.S. Navy.

Some seashore residents and visitors have reported seeing a ghostly airship, or at least its shadow, as far south as Cape May. And it is true that the Hindenburg once cruised along the shoreline to Cape May and back to Lakehurst. On its final fatal voyage, the Hindenburg was delayed in landing at Lakehurst, first by strong headwinds, and later by a thunderstorm. To kill time and entertain his passengers while awaiting good weather at Lakehurst, the Hindenburg's captain Max Pruss took his ship along the coast to Cape May and back.

So if you glimpse a long, torpedo-shaped shadow on a spring afternoon, either in the Lakehurst Triangle or along the seashore as far as south Cape May, look up quickly!

The Phantom Canal Diggers

Ortley Beach, a lovely little seashore community just north of Seaside Heights, is haunted. Not by just one ghost, but by a whole crew of ghosts—a construction crew that seem doomed to keep digging their way across the narrow stretch of sand that is now known as Ortley Beach. The ghostly crew, armed with shovels, is still trying to dig a channel, or canal, across Ortley Beach to connect the Atlantic Ocean on its east with the Silvery Bay section of Barnegat Bay to the west. But as fast and energetically as they dig, the ocean's waves and currents keep filling in their diggings. They must be very frustrated ghosts.

It seems that Mitchell Ortley, who once lived on the beach that now bears his name, was a visionary and ambitious businessman. In the late eighteenth and early nineteenth centuries, Toms River was one of the most important towns in the Jersey Shore region, a busy port for fishing boats and trading ships. To get from Toms River to the open ocean, however, ships had to use Cranberry Inlet, which was located where Seaside Heights now hosts many happy vacationers. What is now Seaside Heights was largely underwater. Cranberry Inlet was a busy waterway—up until 1812, when Mother Nature decided to close the inlet, filling it in with sand. The sailors' loss was future beach lovers' gain.

Mitchell Ortley, like everyone else in the vicinity of Toms River, knew what an unfortunate thing the closing of Cranberry Inlet was for the area's sailors and fishermen. With Cranberry Inlet gone, Toms River's boats and ships now had to detour an additional twelve miles southward to Barnegat Inlet. And not only was Barnegat Inlet farther away and less accessible, but it also was a notoriously tricky channel to navigate. Barnegat richly deserves its name, as it translates from the Dutch as "inlet with large waves or breakers." Large waves might be good news to surfer dudes, but not to sailors.

Ortley's dream was to dig a new inlet across the sandy beach just north of the former Cranberry Inlet. His new shipping channel, to be known as Ortley's Canal, would be closer and easier to use than Barnegat. Ships would pay tolls to use his canal and avoid going twelve miles out of their way to the notorious "large waves" inlet. And the tolls would make Ortley rich.

It was a brilliant idea, so Mitchell hired a construction crew and the men started shoveling sand. As the story goes, they dug and dug for four seasons, until finally it was time to dig out the last few feet of sand between the ocean and bay. The last few shovels of sand were shifted and the canal was open. Success! Ortley and his men went to a nearby tavern to celebrate. The drinks flowed like the ocean tides. Late the next morning, staggering under the fathers of all hangovers, Ortley and his men returned to their new channel to begin construction of the all-important tollbooth. But their new canal was no longer there! The tides and currents had filled it in with beach sand, and all their hard work had been canceled by nature in one night. Ortley's canal had become what you see today—Ortley Beach.

Many local people claim that to this day, one can glimpse sweaty, heavily muscled, and well-tanned workmen digging endlessly at a channel that mysteriously is never cleared of sand. It is best not to approach them, for they most likely are in a foul mood—endlessly frustrated at their task and badly hung over as well.

The Old Seadog's Ghost

The fact that the old seadog is buried on the grounds of the Barnegat Light Life Boat Station probably breaks all kinds of rules and regulations, for this is not an official cemetery. But then, this distinguished member of the U.S. Coast Guard broke the rules all his life and was even honored for always being the exception among his crewmates. For this old seadog, who served almost all of his life aboard the Coast Guard cutter *Campbell,* was a twenty-four-pound, black, brown, and white genuine purebred American mongrel named Sinbad. In his life, he became famous. He once went on a nationwide publicity tour on behalf of his beloved Coast Guard. A movie, *Dog of the Seven Seas,* was made of his life, released in 1947 by Universal Pictures. And many have heard his ghostly barks of comradely greetings to those in military uniform, as well as his frantic woofs warning of ships in trouble at sea.

Sinbad served proudly as the *Campbell*'s mascot from 1937 to 1951. His shipmates believed that Sinbad brought good luck to their ship, and the *Campbell* indeed was lucky. On one occasion during World War II, the cutter bravely tackled an entire "wolfpack" of German subs, which together were hunting down and sinking oil tankers heading for the Raritan Bay refineries. The *Campbell* fought a twelve-hour duel with the subs, finally ramming and sinking one. The cutter was so badly damaged during this battle that the order was given to abandon ship. Sinbad was one of the last coastguardsmen to leave before the ship was taken in tow back to port. She was repaired and sailed again to protect American shipping, and Sinbad was aboard once more.

His shipmates swore that Sinbad sensed danger for the *Campbell* and raised an alarm when another ship was in trouble nearby.

Although no one has actually seen Sinbad's ghost, many have heard his alarm barks at times when, it turned out, a ship was in trouble somewhere off the Jersey coast. And any Coast Guard or Navy personnel passing near his little grave is likely to hear a friendly greeting—especially if they are headed to or from a bar, for Sinbad was a party animal.

Sinbad loved to go drinking with his shipmates when on shore leave. His buddies always bought his drinks. Reportedly, Sinbad would perch up on a barstool just like his friends, happily lapping up a shot of bourbon (he didn't like scotch and would pout if offered one) from a shallow bowl, followed by a beer chaser. And also like his shipmates, Sinbad would have a hangover the next morning. His friends would give him an aspirin, which seemed to help. Whenever the *Campbell* was in port, Sinbad would station himself at the head of the gangway, eager to join his shipmates in a friendly drink, and usually available to help returning drunken friends find their way down to their bunks.

So, whether in military uniform or not, when visiting a bar at the Jersey Shore, have a drink in memory of Sinbad, the littlest sailor. And listen for barking from an unseen dog near the Barnegat Light Life Boat Station.

The Ghosts Drink to St. Francis

If you are ever in a bar on Long Beach Island and witness a local, dressed in rather old-fashioned clothing, raising a glass to St. Francis (often, a lot more than one glass), be careful. You may have encountered a ghost. Or at least, an old-timer who knows a good story.

Famous among the many ships wrecked off Long Beach Island in the mid-nineteenth century was a ship called the *Francis*. The *Francis*, it seems, caught fire off Long Beach while heading for New York from California carrying a valuable cargo of wine and brandy. When the fire broke out, her captain decided to hug the coastline in the hope that if the *Francis* had to be abandoned, the crew could swim ashore. The *Francis* hugged the coast a bit too closely and ran aground on a sandbar. Her crew did make it safely ashore.

Then, as the *Francis* broke apart in the waves, cask after fifty-gallon cask began to wash ashore. As the islanders soon discovered, much of the *Francis*'s cargo eventually washed up on the beach. Fine wines and brandies filled most casks, accompanied by barrels of the best salted Pacific salmon. It was party time! It is reported that every household got its share of California's finest. Even the local Methodist minister was gifted with some top-quality wines and spirits. Everyone shared, or almost everyone. The local railroad stationmaster secured a particularly large cask of brandy and refused to share it with his friends and neighbors. He locked his cask inside a freight car on a siding near the station. When he went to sample his prize the next day, the cask was empty. During the night, thirsty islanders had drilled a hole up through the freight car's floor and into the wooden cask, draining it.

For many years afterward, local drunks were said to be "praying to St. Francis," and a common islander toast was to raise a glass to St. Francis. There are those who claim that ghostly drinkers to this day still loudly salute St. Francis as they tip back a glass or two of "spirits."

The Ghost Beacons of the Tuckerton Tower

It seems to happen in times of international crises, when war involving the United States is threatened. Local residents and pilots of low-flying planes report seeing flashing red beacons warning aircraft away from the 862-foot-high radio transmission tower near Tuckerton. There is nothing unusual about the warning lights— except that the Tuckerton Tower was demolished in 1955.

The Tuckerton Tower was built by the imperial German government, operating through an alleged private company, in 1912. At the time, it was one of the most powerful radio transmitters in the world, capable of exchanging messages with Germany and German naval vessels in the Atlantic. Operating with the highest voltage of any radio station in the world, the Tuckerton Tower was used solely for commercial messages, claimed the Germans.

But many historians believe that German operatives managed to send a coded message on May 7, 1915, to submarines operating in European waters to "get Lucy," meaning sink the British passenger liner *Lusitania*. The *Lusitania* was torpedoed off the coast of Ireland, with a loss of 1,198 lives, 124 of them American. This incident was credited with swinging American public opinion against Germany. The U.S. government refuses to either deny or confirm that the Tuckerton Tower transmitted the fatal order to the German submarine U-20 about the *Lusitania*. The day after America declared war on Germany, April 6, 1917, the U.S. military took complete control of the tower, operating it for military communications until 1948. It was torn down seven years later.

Do the long-demolished tower's ghostly warning lights flash still when war is on the horizon? Some New Jerseyans think so.

The Sailing Ship on Rails

Seeing ghosts can be a frightening, even terrifying, experience. Sometimes the apparition is nonthreatening, perhaps even well-intentioned. But a few ghostly sightings are so bizarre, so unusual, that the observers rarely tell anyone about it, as they doubt their eyes and fear that others will doubt their sanity. Or at least, their sobriety.

Such is the case with the sailing vessel that appeared to cruise serenely across the marshy bayshores near Tuckerton. Why—and how—does a ship under sail manage to move across land? Those who have seen this specter assume that they've had at least one drink too many. Even ghosts should follow some rules. How can a ship sail across land?

Well, for those who believe in ghosts, the vision is based on historical fact. It seems that in the early 1880s, the railroad decided to bypass Tuckerton, and a length of track leading from the bayshore was abandoned by the railroad company. Some local oystermen, looking for an easy way to take their catch to market, rigged sails on an old flatcar, and the Tuckerton sailcar railway was in operation. This ingenuous contraption ran—or rather, sailed—for a few years, then was crashed into a ditch by pranksters in 1886. It never sailed again—except as a ghost.

New Jersey's "Paul Revere"

The runner appears to be panting from exertion as he races along the banks of the Mullica River near its exit into Great Bay. He is not an ordinary jogger, for he is wearing the simple clothing of a

Colonial-era fisherman. And he is not living, but a ghost. He can't stop, as he is running not just for his own life, but to save many lives. His name was Nathaniel Cowperthwaite, and though he is not as famous as Paul Revere, he faced the same type of desperate mission. And today his ghost still pounds breathlessly along the riverbanks, hurrying to warn the patriots that the British are coming.

It was the spring of 1778, and British general Sir Henry Clinton was angry. American privateers were harassing British ships along the New Jersey coast. The small, fast ships would slip out of the rivers and bays behind the sandy beaches, attack and capture British merchant ships, and sell their cargoes to help finance the Revolution. The previous year, the British ship *Venus* had been seized by the Americans, who used the cargo to reprovision Washington's army. Determined to wipe out this "nest of Jersey pirates," Clinton sent seven hundred soldiers aboard ships to attack the American privateers. They were also to destroy the Batsto Ironworks, where the patriots were making cannonballs.

The British expedition burned thirty ships at Tuckerton—prize ships captured by the Americans. Then they captured local fisherman Nathaniel Cowperthwaite and made him an offer he couldn't refuse: Guide them to Batsto or they would kill him. Nathaniel knew those waters well. Craftily pretending to cooperate, he piloted the British right onto a submerged sandbar, where they were grounded. He then slipped overboard, swam to shore, and started running to warn his fellow patriots.

He did succeed in warning some Americans of the approaching British forces, but one advance outpost was overrun before the exhausted fisherman could get to them, and thirty Americans were massacred.

And so the ghost of Nathaniel, frantic to warn others, continues to run endlessly along the riverbanks. "The British are coming! The British are coming!"

South Shore

The Ghost with the Most Diamonds

Every now and then, evening strollers along Atlantic City's famed Boardwalk catch a quick view of an immaculately dressed, obese older man riding along the Boardwalk in an old-fashioned wicker rolling chair pushed by a black attendant. Oddly, he seems to be wearing flamboyantly large diamonds—a tie stickpin and several gaudy rings. But when they try to get a closer look at this glittering apparition, the image disappears as though the man, his chair, and his servant have all simply evaporated. Many who've had this experience think they've seen the ghost of Diamond Jim Brady.

When the future millionaire and bon vivant was born in New York City on August 12, 1856, his parents named him James Buchanan Brady. Superstitiously, they thought that naming the child after the newly elected president of the United States would guarantee him a bright future. President Buchanan, it turned out, was not regarded as a particularly successful president, as he did nothing to prevent the coming Civil War, which confronted his successor, Abraham Lincoln. But James Buchanan was a self-made rich man, one of the most successful lawyers of his day, so maybe it was his moneymaking skills that rubbed off on James Buchanan Brady.

Born to a poor family, Brady got his first job as a hotel bellboy. Soon, however, his jovial, larger-than-life personality, brimming with fellowship and self-confidence, led him to a successful career selling railroad equipment. One of the first to see that steel railroad cars would quickly displace those made of wood, he organized the Pressed Steel Car Company and made a fortune, one so large that he earned the nickname "Diamond Jim" by collecting $2 million worth of diamond jewelry. He said that he had a different set of diamond jewelry for each day of the week, as he believed it was bad luck to wear the same diamonds every day. He wore a lot of diamonds, but never thirteen at once, as he was superstitious.

Diamond Jim loved Atlantic City. He had his penthouse at the Shelbourne Hotel outfitted with gold bathroom fixtures. He ate and drank the best of everything—in large quantities. His immense weight and gout made it painful to walk, so he loved to be pushed along the Boardwalk in his rolling chair, cigar and glass of champagne in hand. He had one last rolling chair ride, at least as a living soul, on April 12, 1917. The next day, the thirteenth, his unlucky day, he was dead.

But many believe that his ghost still rides in a rolling chair along the boards. If you see his spirit on the Boardwalk, raise a glass of champagne to his memory—he'd appreciate that. The best French champagne, of course.

Taps at the Cape May Point Bunker

The faint sounds of a bugle can barely be heard above the surf. The calls are coming from a military installation, so why would people be surprised that they can hear taps being played at sundown? Because the military site in question has stood derelict for decades.

At Cape May Point State Park, at the southernmost tip of New Jersey, a huge pile of concrete perched on a forest of wooden pilings stands high above the surrounding waves. Built in 1942, its purpose was to help protect the entrance to Delaware Bay against enemy warships. Although German submarines did operate off New Jersey in World War II, no enemy surface ships ever showed up, so the bunker's six-inch guns were never fired in battle.

The structure is built of six-foot-thick concrete walls and roof, covered in turf to camouflage it from the air. When constructed, it was nine hundred feet from the waves, but erosion along the beach has since stranded the bunker out in the water.

In addition to hearing bugle calls from the abandoned fortification, some observers claim to have seen mysterious lights on it at night. Are World War II gunners still on guard against German battleships that never appeared?

The Ghost Who Is So Proud

Beautifully dressed in mid-nineteenth-century finery, including a black tailcoat and top hat, this phantom strolls the streets and beach of Atlantic City. The figure usually is seen only shortly after dawn. Early strollers on the Boardwalk are among those who will glimpse the seemingly out-of-place Victorian gentleman, so formally dressed in a town where a T-shirt is practically semiformal.

But the mysterious figure really is not out of place in a historical sense. Longtime residents of Atlantic City figure that the ghost must be their own Dr. Jonathan Pitney, the physician known as the "father" of Atlantic City. This ghost threatens no one. He strolls along with a proud, satisfied smile on his face as he views the beautiful skyline of casino hotels, gleaming in the early-morning rays of the sun. He has reason to smile: He is like a father expressing his satisfaction that his offspring has become so successful in maturity.

The good doctor always had faith in the city's growth, and his daybreak inspection tours show that his vision of a prosperous future for Absecon Island has come to pass. Dr. Pitney was a dreamer, but also a man of action. He was a prominent and influential citizen of the area, and one with some money to invest, so others listened to him. Where others might have seen only an almost uninhabited sandbar, desolate in winter and plagued by green flies and mosquitoes in summer, Dr. Pitney saw a great beach resort that would serve Philadelphians looking for some fun in the sun. Absecon Island would become a playground for millions, he thought, as soon as vacationers were able to reach the seashore quickly and inexpensively. What was needed was a railroad, so he helped organize the Camden and Atlantic Railroad to bring would-be beachgoers to his island.

Dr. Pitney believed that fortunes could be made from real estate in the new resort he envisioned. And he was right. Oceanfront land that he and his friends bought for $17.50 an acre in 1854 now goes for $2,000 or more per square foot. No wonder Jonathan Pitney's ghost has a satisfied smile on his face. Wouldn't you?

The Haunted Cottage

The small cottage sits on a quiet backroad near the tiny community of Cape May Point, at the southernmost tip of New Jersey. Its unpainted cedar shingles are in poor condition, and there is a general air of neglect. The house is available for rent but often stands empty. There are no close neighbors.

A married couple from Philadelphia, both enthusiastic bird-watchers, once rented the place for a week in May. The old cottage was not very handy to the beaches, but the "point" of New Jersey is a prime location for bird-watching, so much so that the state's branch of the National Audubon Society sponsors a "world series of birding" here each May.

And so our two bird-watchers, spotting an ad in a Philadelphia newspaper, rented the place sight unseen at what seemed an attractive price even for the prebeach season. The ghostly harassment started the first night, but only in a small way. Tucked into bed in the upstairs front bedroom, the couple heard what sounded like footsteps—just a few—on the stairs nearby. As the sounds soon ceased, they concluded that it was just the normal creaks and groans of old wood responding to wind and temperature change. They slept well.

On their second night, however, the sounds of footsteps lasted longer and were more distinct. When the husband bravely opened the bedroom door to investigate, there was nothing to be seen. The next morning, though, the heavy bolt on the front door, which could be opened or closed only from inside, was in the open position, though they had firmly closed and bolted the door the night before.

Now alarmed, the couple decided that someone must be trying to frighten them, and that person had succeeded. They searched the small house thoroughly, looking for hidden speakers, gadgets, or electronics that could explain the mysterious noises they'd heard. They could find nothing.

They went to bed that next night with a great deal of apprehension, and their fears were justified. The unexplained noises began getting louder and louder. The sounds of footsteps were accompanied by definite vibrations on the steps. The locked and bolted door slammed open and shut repeatedly. The temperature dropped abruptly, reaching freezing in a matter of seconds. Loud moans now accompanied the ghostly footsteps. Terrified, the couple packed their bags and fled the cottage in the middle of the night. Fearing ridicule, they described their encounter with a ghost to friends only after many years of silence.

Reasoning with the Ghost

Although the house was over a hundred years old, it had a lot of old-fashioned charm and was in a great location in the highly desirable Ocean City. The family who had just moved in were pleased with their new home—that is, until the ghost made its presence known.

Not everyone in the household was aware of the ghost at first. The mother, and then the father, noticed that their teenage daughter was reluctant to go into the living room by herself, especially at night. She refused to discuss her avoidance of that room, claiming only that something made her uneasy. After several months, the teenager finally admitted that she had seen a ghost but was afraid to admit it, concerned that her parents would think that she was crazy or on drugs. "There's a strange woman in the living room," she reported, "and she looks very unhappy."

And then stranger things began to happen—doors slamming shut and lights going on or off by themselves. Then, late one night, the family's toddler awakened everybody by screaming. The little boy, plainly terrified by something, could only point to the door of his room, wide-eyed and trembling. The father decided to sleep on the floor of his son's bedroom for the rest of the night. He was awakened by a tapping on his shoulder, but there was no one else in the room other than the toddler, asleep in his crib. The door was closed, though it had been left open. He couldn't get back to sleep.

Although neither adult had seen the ghost, the whole family now was convinced that the house was haunted. The parents' reaction was a little unusual, however. They sat down with their children in the living room where the daughter had seen the phantom. "Look," the father said, speaking to the ghost, "you seem to live here, or at least exist here. Well, now we live here too. Why can't we share the house peacefully? We mean you no harm. Let's agree not to bother one another."

This reasoning with the spirit appeared to work. When, after a few months, the apparition again is seen or sounds are heard, another family meeting is held to appeal to the ghost—to agree to quietly share the space—and then annoying manifestations cease, at least for another few months.

So try reasoning with your ghost, if you have one. It just might work.

Reliving Bessie's Happiest Evening

It is common for people to revisit, in memory, cherished moments from their past. Ghosts, too, sometimes appear to relive happier times—again and again. Such seems to be the case with the gloriously self-confident ghost of a young woman seen along Cape May's Boardwalk. Sometimes, it is said, the ghost even dances by herself, as if absorbed in a magical moment.

Some longtime residents of Cape May claim to have occasionally seen a shimmering, pale figure of a beautiful young woman strolling along the seafront very late on early-summer nights. She appears to be radiantly happy, and so she should be, for she has been reliving a happy occasion: She was just the star of an old-fashioned coming-out party. Early in the twentieth century, these lavish dinner dances were customarily held to formally introduce young women to society as young adults now eligible for dating. This particular spirit's party had been held at the elite Colonial Hotel. Renamed the Inn at Cape May, it still stands on Beach Avenue.

Though Bessie Warfield, as she was called in childhood (her real first name was a family name, and not particularly feminine), grew up as a boardinghouse cook's daughter, she early determined that someday she would live like a princess in a fairy tale. Her hometown was Baltimore, and in keeping with long-established tradition dating from before the Civil War, Cape May was the preferred seaside retreat of Baltimoreans with social pretensions. And pretension is the key word, as the slender, rather boyish-looking, newly adult "member of society" had little going for her besides a driving ambition. As a small child, she had undergone an embarrassing, even humiliating, move from a luxurious home to a run-down boarding-house. Her mother, the daughter of a socially prominent couple, had gone from riches to rags following the untimely death of her wealthy husband.

Why does Bessie's ghost wander happily along Cape May's seafront, when later life saw her living mostly in France and New York City? Perhaps, in the afterglow of her first grown-up and evidently successful party, Cape May was the last time she experienced innocent joy at life's prospects before her. This Baltimore girl, who no doubt had scrimped and saved for her coming-out party on Cape May's seafront drive for months, was to achieve both fame and notoriety following her third marriage. She was the woman for whom a king gave up his throne; many admired and envied her, but many others hated her. Her real name? Wallis Warfield Spenser Simpson Windsor, a.k.a. the Duchess of Windsor.

The Phantom Lifeguard

A couple visiting Sea Isle City told this story of their encounter with a lifeguard—one who had been dead for years.

It was a sunny weekday afternoon in late September. The couple owned a summer cottage at Sea Isle and had come to close it up for winter. Winter seemed a long way off that day, however. Weather in late September and early October is one of the best-kept secrets of the Jersey Shore. Days can be warm but not brutally hot, the humidity is lower than in summer, and the water temperatures are still comfortable, as the ocean retains its summer heat longer than the land. Better yet, the crowds are gone, and there's no difficulty finding a parking spot or a prime location for your beach blanket. One more quick dip in the inviting ocean seemed to the couple like a good way to cap a delightful season.

The pair waded out to waist depth, playing in the surf and enjoying the otherwise empty beach. But it wasn't completely empty, as they soon discovered. A lifeguard in traditional red trunks and tank top blew his whistle, gesturing at a rock and concrete jetty to which the couple had gotten too close, as they had unknowingly drifted with the alongshore current.

As they waded back to the beach, they noticed that the lifeguard was gone. They packed up their beach blanket and headed back to their car. A local policeman, seeing their wet bathing suits, admonished them that swimming was not encouraged in the off-season, as there were no lifeguards on duty. "But there was a lifeguard," they replied. "In fact, he warned us away from the jetty." The officer told them that no guards were on duty that late in the year. When the couple described the lifeguard, the officer was puzzled. "That sounds like Captain Jack," he said. "He was in charge of the beach patrol for years—but he died about ten years ago." Apparently the spirit of the conscientious lifeguard was still looking out for the safety of visitors to "his" beach.

The Helpful Little Dog

Old-timers in Atlantic City swear they've seen a little mongrel, once the city's most famous dog, still standing on street corners downtown, waiting for a taxi. A dog belonging to a bartender at a popular local hangout was well known as the friend and protector of drunks. When his master's customers had had a few too many, Night Life, as he was known, would help them walk home safely. He would wait until traffic was clear before allowing his human friends to cross the street. When his mission was accomplished, he would return to the bar, perhaps to assist another inebriate home. When Night Life's guide-dog chores took him far from his master's bar, he would simply hail a cab! All the night-owl cab drivers knew him and gladly would give him a lift when they spotted the "drunk's friend" waiting patiently at a street corner.

When Night Life died, the locals took up a collection to bury him in style at a mainland pet cemetery. But many claim that late at night on downtown street corners, the ghost of Night Life still waits to guide drunks across the street. And he hopes for a taxi to stop and give him a lift back to the bar.

The Ghost of the Tragic Chambermaid

A college student working a part-time seasonal job as a security guard once had a horrific encounter with a ghost in a Cape May hotel. The Admiral Hotel, built in the early twentieth century, sits at the northeastern end of Beach Avenue, overlooking the beach. In the dead of winter, the grand old hotel, with its marble lobby, brass stair railings, and inlaid paneling, was virtually empty. The student had been hired as a night watchman, a position that should have been an unadventurous, not to say boring, job providing him with ample opportunity to catch up on studying while looking after the seasonally empty hotel.

One night in January, with a gale blowing outside, the watchman took the elegant brass elevator up to the top floor, which was occupied by a restaurant and lounge with a fabulous scenic view of the beach and ocean. As the old elevator rose slowly, it began to fill with a mystifying cold, white fog. This had never happened before. When the elevator doors opened at the top floor, he saw that the whole lounge was filled with fog. In the faint glow of the security lights, a body was visible, hanging by the neck from a ceiling beam. As the watchman stared in horror, the corpse's eyes snapped open. This panicked the poor student guard, who ducked back into the elevator in a cold sweat. As the elevator descended, the swirling mist gradually evaporated.

When he reported the experience to his supervisor, the night watchman learned that the apparition had appeared before, always on the same date. It was the anniversary of a young hotel chambermaid's suicide. No one ever discovered her reason for hanging herself, nor why she chose to do this in the beautiful top-floor lounge. The student guard soon afterward left his unexpectedly terrifying job.

The Ghost in the Elephant

This could happen only at the Jersey Shore. Not only does a giant elephant stand on the beach looking out to sea, but the elephant also may be host to a ghost.

Lucy, the Margate elephant, stands sixty-five feet tall. Constructed in 1881 by a real estate developer, she was built of wood, with a "skin" made of hammered tin sheets. Her job was to attract attention and she did well at that. Originally used as a real estate office, Lucy also served as a tavern, hotel, and private home before being rescued from decay and restored as a museum in 1970.

Lucy's resident ghost has been spotted in the early-morning hours peacefully lounging in the howdah, an open-air, covered passenger box like those that real Indian elephants once carried on their backs. The ghost seems to be looking out to sea while sipping a tall drink. Some speculate that Lucy's ghost is that of an old bartender who worked there long ago, when the old elephant was a tavern. It had been his habit, after closing and cleaning up, to have a quiet drink on top of Lucy while enjoying the cool night breezes. No one has ever seen the ghost during Lucy's daytime museum hours, however, so enjoy your tour of America's only walk-through wood and tin elephant.

Heading Back to a Safe Harbor

The ghost ship appears infrequently at the Great Egg Harbor Inlet, between Longport and Ocean City. Her flag flying proudly from her stern, the antique wooden sailing ship is believed to be the ghostly image of the U.S. Navy's fighting frigate *Intrepid*, heading at last to a safe harbor—Somers Point, the home of her heroic commander, Master Commandant Richard Somers. Sightings of the *Intrepid*, under full sail, with cannons bristling from her oaken flanks, seem to occur most often when the nation is at war.

The *Intrepid* and Somers earned their enduring fame in military history during the 1804 American stand against Turkish pirates based in what is now Libya. The ancient port of Tripoli (as sung about in the *Marine Hymn*) was a nest of pirates that the United States determined to fight rather than pay blackmail tribute.

Richard Somers was the son of the seafaring family that founded Somers Point on the bay behind Ocean City. In the attack on Tripoli's pirate fleet, Somers was to sail the *Intrepid* into the midst of the pirates and then set her on fire before abandoning his ship. The plan was that the *Intrepid*, loaded with explosives, would blow up, taking a lot of pirate ships with her. But the *Intrepid* caught fire and blew up somewhat prematurely, killing Somers and his crew before they could escape, though it did also destroy many pirate ships. In commemoration of Somers's patriotic sacrifice, the U.S. Navy ever since has included a warship named *Intrepid.*

But the ghostly *Intrepid* still sails as well, perpetually heading for a safe harbor at Somers's hometown after carrying out her dangerous mission. A few local fishermen have even seen the *Intrepid* at night, glowing with an eerie greenish white light as she sails toward the inlet leading home.

The Case of the Terrified Cat

Be warned: The story of how this ghost came to be is even scarier than the ghost. It is the ghost of a cat—but not a whole cat. This truly terrifying apparition is of a cat's head without a body.

Back near the bay in Wildwood, in a neighborhood of small, rather shabby houses, a very unusual phantom has been seen, mostly on moonlit nights, when moonlight is eerily reflected in the glowing, green eyes of a ghostly cat. The cat's head screams terror, not only with unearthly howling, but also with bared teeth, flattened ears, and every hair standing on end, combined to communicate pure fright and concentrated hate.

The evil act that produced this angry restless ghost is stomach-churning. The legend is that many years ago, a neighborhood boy of about twelve, who showed the classic symptoms of a psychopath, took satisfaction in cruelly tormenting small animals. His rage and indifference to the suffering of his victims eventually culminated in a genuinely horrific act. He dug a shallow hole in a backyard lawn, and then buried a stray cat up to its neck. The next step involved a power lawn mower. People still shudder when retelling the tale. The boy, the story goes, was locked away in the violent ward of a mental hospital. The cat's ghost—or rather, the apparition of its severed head—still roams late at night. This is the stuff of nightmares, so run—don't just walk—away if you spy the disembodied head of a cat some night in Wildwood.

The Ghost Who Loves to Tango

Garden Pier, near the northeast end of Atlantic City's beachfront and Boardwalk, has had a hard life. Now occupied by the Atlantic City Historical Museum and Arts Center, the present pier is just the stub of a once grander pier, as the ruins of its concrete foundations at the seaward end can testify.

There are those who swear that on moonlit nights, an elegantly slender, handsome young man can be seen dancing the tango with one eager partner after another. The suave figure with hypnotic black eyes flashing as he dances is thought to be the ghost of none other than the 1920s movie star Rudolph Valentino. For the great Valentino, before he headed west to Hollywood in 1918, once held what for him at the time was a dream job—giving dancing lessons to adoring women in the ballroom that once stood at the ocean end of Garden Pier.

The future idol of women around the world was born Rodolfo O'Antonguela in Castellaneta, Italy, on May 6, 1895. His family emigrated to America, where young Rodolfo held a variety of menial jobs, such as dishwasher and gardener, before signing on as a dance instructor in Atlantic City. He had a natural grace, and his good looks had the ladies lining up to pay to learn the newly popular, and very romantic, tango.

It was on Garden Pier that Rudy first realized that he attracted women like a magnet. He headed for Hollywood, where he used his middle name, Valentino, as his stage name. In his first starring role, in *The Four Horseman of the Apocalypse* (1921), he proved that he could act. But it was his roles as a hot-blooded Arab "bad boy" that made millions of women his wannabe love slaves as they thrilled to *The Sheik* (1921), *Blood and Sand* (1923), and *Son of the Sheik* (1926).

Valentino died suddenly on August 23, 1926, in New York City, but his spirit lives on—not only in films, but also in the exotic and erotic dancing style he first practiced on Garden Pier in Atlantic City. Today his ghost, a sinuously graceful body dressed all in black, still glides across a phantom dance floor that washed out to sea in a hurricane decades ago.

King Nummy's Mummy

Legend has it that Nummy's Island, in the bay behind North Wildwood at the edge of Hereford Inlet, is haunted. Nummy's is hardly worthy of being called an island. It is more like a little patch of marsh grass, barely above high tide.

The island was named for "King" Nummy, the last chief of a local group of Unalachtigo Indians, which were the southernmost band of the Lenni-Lenape tribe. "Lenni-Lenape" translates as "the people" or the "original people." Each local band of Lenni-Lenape had its own totem, a symbol that was thought to be the essence of its culture and identity. The totem was an image to live up to. The Minsi of northern New Jersey, for example, selected the wolf, which symbolizes boldness, courage, and cunning, as their totem. The Unalachtigo's totem was the turkey. Although the contemporary image of the turkey is one of massive stupidity, a wild turkey is a crafty bird, not at all easy to find, as hunters can testify. To the Unalachtigo, their turkey totem symbolized a creature that survived through its wits, not its claws or fangs. Strategy, not physical strength, was the wild turkey's survival advantage. As the group's sachem, or chief, Nummy was expected to display the cunning caution of their totem. But in this he failed, for he clearly was outsmarted by the Europeans. His group of Indians lost its land and was forced to move westward.

"King" Nummy traded away the Indians' coastal lands, including the offshore beaches, because Nummy considered them relatively valueless. What use were they, except for summer and fall excursions to catch fish and dig for clams? In negotiating with the British colonists, Nummy made a big mistake—one that a good lawyer would have advised against: Nummy didn't get in writing what he thought was an agreement that the Indians, even after selling their land, could continue to hunt and fish there. In the Indians' way of thinking, the fish, shellfish, and game birds and animals were separate from the land itself. But not to the Europeans.

When the Unalachtigo realized that Nummy's deal with the British had traded away their food supply, they had to abandon the area. They also abandoned Nummy, whom they now sconed as an inept, not very smart leader. And so Nummy, rejected by his tribe and scorned by the British, retreated to a small, marshy island in which the colonists had no interest. The former chief lived out his life in solitude on his little island, cursing his own lack of cunning.

It is said that King Nummy's body was mummified by the hot sun and salt air as it lay unburied after he died. So today Nummy's mummy roams the marshes and beaches of his last refuge, cursing the whites who outsmarted him several centuries ago. Beware, for his is a hostile spirit.

The Ghostly Tap Dancer

Many remember hearing the rhythmic tap-tap-tapping sounds along Atlantic City's Boardwalk, usually late at night or early in the morning. The musical taps can be heard best when the Boardwalk is almost deserted, which is to say, only at odd hours in the off-season. Distinctly different from the regularity of the nearby surf, the tapping sounds are reminiscent of a uniquely American art form: tap dancing. With a little imagination, you can almost hear the music accompanying the taps.

Hearing, rather than seeing, ghosts is not all that unusual. Are people who are hearing a rhythmic pattern of taps along the Boardwalk experiencing an encounter with a ghost? Or is the tapping merely the random creaks of the boards responding to temperature and humidity changes and the impact of many human feet?

Those familiar with Atlantic City's history, particularly its show-business history, are convinced that one of the greatest tap dancers to ever appear onstage in Atlantic City, and elsewhere, is still expressing his zest for life and great satisfaction in entertaining his audience. The intricate patterns of taps heard on the Boardwalk may be the ghostly curtain calls of a man who was one of the greatest tap dancers of all time—though he only had one leg!

Clayton Bates was born in 1907 in Fountain Inn, South Carolina, to a poor black family, and little Clayton didn't enjoy many of life's luxuries. But nothing could discourage his natural sense of joy in life, and he expressed it through dancing. At age five, he was dancing for pennies in local barbershops. By age twelve, he was working the graveyard shift at a cotton mill, feeding cottonseed into a machine that pressed oil from the seed. One night he fell into the press—an accident that severed his left leg below the knee and cost him two fingers off his right hand.

A leg amputation would have ended the dancing career of a less determined man, but Clayton hammered a metal tap onto his wooden leg, and a legendary star was born. "Peg Leg" Bates soon had star billing on Broadway, at the age of nineteen. He appeared onstage with the great Count Basie and toured as far away as Australia with Louis Armstrong. He was featured at Radio City Music Hall and was the first African American to appear on television's *Ed Sullivan Show*, in 1950. Ed had him back twenty-two times. But his favorite place to perform was in Atlantic City, where he first starred at the Club Harlem in 1943. A great showman, Bates had his wooden legs made in an assortment of colors, with matching tuxes and top hats. The irrepressible dancer performed almost continually until his death in December 1998 at age ninety-one.

It is said that some of his greatest performances were for free. He volunteered countless times to entertain wounded servicemen during World War II, when some Atlantic City hotels were used as convalescent centers for soldiers and sailors recovering from surgery—such as amputations.

In life, Peg Leg Bates showed an unconquerable spirit—a classic tale of talent and determination overcoming seemingly a insurmountable handicap. Perhaps that world-class spirit just won't die. So listen carefully next time you hear joyful tapping sounds along Atlantic City's Boardwalk.

The Witch and the Lizard

An old story claims that Cape May once was home to a witch named Peggy Clevenger. Peggy lived by herself and rarely socialized with her neighbors. Many believed that the lonely old woman was a witch who, as the occasion warranted, could turn herself into a rabbit or lizard. The gossip was that Peggy had a stocking filled with gold hidden somewhere in her house.

One day when Peggy appeared to be absent, a neighbor, driven by curiosity about the alleged witch and her golden treasure, decided to sneak over to her house and look around. The trespassing neighbor's path was blocked by a large, green lizard. It would not move, even after the neighbor threw a stone at its head, so the nosy neighbor retreated.

The next day, Peggy Clevenger appeared with a black eye in the same place that the stone had struck the lizard. No neighbors ever tried to approach Peggy's house again.

Later, Peggy was murdered in her bed, apparently by thieves looking for her gold. It is believed that the gold was never found, but that a big lizard still guards the ruins of the witch's house. Those who challenge the lizard soon suffer a series of accidents. Is it just bad luck or vengeful witchcraft?

The Colonel's Ghostly Inspection Tours

The apparition marches determinedly along the roadside, carefully inspecting the land and buildings, often shaking his head in disgust at any untidiness. The ghostly figure is an impressive sight, dressed in the parade uniform of a full colonel of the Civil War era, wearing a plumed hat and carrying a dress sword. And he is African American.

The ghost that periodically goes on inspection tours in the vicinity of McKee City is that of the little community's namesake, Colonel John McKee. McKee City, a rather grand name for a rural community, now developing quickly thanks to its location, flanks a traffic circle on the old Black Horse Pike (U.S. Route 322) on the mainland behind Atlantic City. Once known as Racetrack Circle, the area now is the location of the Hamilton Mall shopping center.

The colonel would be proud that his vision of a prosperous community of small farms has become a major center of commerce. He bet his life savings on that particular location having a bright future.

John McKee was born in Alexandria, Virginia, in 1821. In 1823, he moved to Philadelphia, where he soon owned a thriving restaurant. A Civil War hero, McKee was the first black officer in the Pennsylvania National Guard. McKee was a successful businessman, and he and his wife soon owned an entire block of houses in Philadelphia. He got interested in real estate development in South Jersey and ended up owning four thousand acres adjacent to the railroad that connected Philadelphia with Atlantic City, then a booming new resort. The colonel divided much of his land into small farms, which he leased to both blacks and whites. McKee loved order and neatness, and his tenants were required to maintain their properties in perfect condition or lose their leases. His leases included detailed directions about where to plant trees, for example.

His ultimate dream, never carried out, was to found a military college to educate boys of all races as future officers. When he died on April 6, 1902, he left his fortune to the Philadelphia Catholic Diocese to fund scholarships in his name. In 1971, the value of his legacy was estimated at $1.25 million.

The Peace-Loving Ghost of Cape May

Was Abigail Hughes a coward or a peacemaker? It all depends on your viewpoint.

During the War of 1812, the story goes, Cape May residents were terrified at the sight of a British man-of-war anchoring offshore. The large frigate bristled with two rows of cannons, every one aimed broadside at the little town. The townspeople had only one cannon, a big gun known as Long Tom. When British soldiers climbed into barges and headed for shore, the citizens dragged Long Tom to the beach and prepared to fire on the invaders.

But a local housewife, Abigail Hughes, disagreed with the desperate attempt to defend the little town. She tied herself across the muzzle of the cannon, claiming that Cape May had more to lose than gain by firing on the approaching soldiers. If Long Tom were fired, surely the British warship would let loose a mighty broadside from its dozens of cannons, demolishing the town. It would be a very unequal fight, one that the Americans surely would lose.

Cooler heads sided with Abigail, and Long Tom remained silent. The soldiers, it turned out, marched right past Cape May, went to the nearby bayshore, and pillaged Town Bank and Fishing Creek before returning to their ship and sailing away.

Was Abigail Hughes a coward or a savior? The answer might depend on whether you ask Cape May's relieved citizens or the bayshore villages' burned-out patriots.

The ghost of Abigail Hughes is said to appear along the seafront in times of war, still trying to dissuade her fellow townspeople from firing the first shot. Cape May never again has been invaded, except by tourists. And there is a Hughes Street in Cape May to this day.

Captain Kidd's Brigantine Treasure

Captain Kidd got around. His "business," after all, required travel. One of the most famous of pirates, Kidd started his career on the side of the angels, or at least the right side of the law. He was a British sea captain who had been granted letters of marque by his majesty's government. That meant that as a private citizen rather than a naval officer, he was authorized to track down, fight, and capture pirate ships or any other enemies of the Crown. And as a privateer, he did pursue and seize pirate ships. But the authorities back in London accused him of attacking and looting nonpirate ships as well. Kidd claimed that he had done no wrong, and that this really was a dispute about the government's share of captured pirate treasure. Nevertheless, he was tried at the Old Bailey Court in London in 1701, found guilty, and hanged in chains at the nearby Tilbury Fort. His body was allowed to slowly rot in an iron cage as a warning to others.

Among the several places along the Jersey Shore said to have been visited by Captain Kidd is Brigantine. Although the captain's ghost has been spotted at numerous locations in coastal New Jersey, it is the ghost of Kidd's first mate, Timothy Jones, who haunts Brigantine Beach.

The story is that Captain Kidd and his crew had buried a treasure chest on Brigantine. Like all sailors familiar with the sandy islands along the New Jersey coast, Kidd had observed that the waves and currents continually moved sand, reshaping the islands, opening and closing inlets, and generally rearranging the shore. He was worried that he had buried his treasure too close to the waves, and that several of his crewmembers knew exactly where it was hidden and might try to claim it.

So Captain Kidd and Timothy Jones rowed ashore one moonless night to dig up and rebury the treasure in a safer location. They had an argument, which Kidd settled by killing his first mate. Jones ended up buried atop the treasure chest. His ghost now sits at the burial site, sharpening his sword, waiting for the treacherous captain to return for the treasure and face the vengeance of his murdered mate. Don't try to dig up the treasure—Jones thinks it is his alone.

Pirate Ghosts at Cape May Point

Pirates used to love hanging out at the Jersey Shore. Their reasons had to do with geography. First, there was the geography of opportunity; the Jersey coast was close to busy shipping lanes. Second, there was the geography of hideouts—places to hide from the law, rest, and reprovision their ships with food and fresh water. And the pirates also considered the geography of stashing away treasure in handy locations for future retrieval, but without too many curious neighbors around.

In the heyday of pirates—the eighteenth and early nineteenth centuries—just as now, the Jersey coast witnessed many ships bound to or from the great ports of New York and Philadelphia. The rich cargoes naturally attracted pirates, just as fat rabbits attract eagles. Much of the Jersey Shore at the time was almost empty of people—people who might spot the pirates coming ashore to replenish food and water supplies, bury treasure, and hide from pursuing naval vessels. The many small inlets and tidal creeks were favorite hiding places of pirates. New Jersey and pirates—perfect together!

Pirates, like everyone else, needed a supply of fresh water. They couldn't drink salt water, and fresh water stored in casks didn't age well—after a few weeks, the water tasted like a skunk had drowned in it. So they periodically rowed ashore in search of fresh water, which wasn't available everywhere. A favorite pirate watering hole was Lake Lily, near the beach at Cape May Point.

The infamous Captain Kidd is supposed to have used Lake Lily so routinely that local folks grew used to the appearance there of pirates. And the spirits of Captain Kidd and his men are said to still show up, just as watchful as the pirates once were in life.

At the time of the pirates, many New Jersey law enforcement officials believed, rightly or wrongly, that the men simply bribed local people not to report their comings and goings. It is said that the pirates paid generously for food and supplies. Captain Kidd also spread the word that talkative heads would be chopped off with a sword. The frequent and unreported pirate shopping trips at Cape May Point grew so notorious that the governor of New Jersey personally led a raid in 1699. He captured four pirates, who

confessed to their crimes, and confiscated a quantity of gold, amber, coral, and silk.

So don't worry if you spot some pirate ghosts. If you ignore them, they'll ignore you—probably.

The Ghosts of Absecon Light

Absecon Lighthouse, in Atlantic City's inlet section, is haunted. But unlike most ghost stories, rather than being the scene of just one ghost's appearances, the lighthouse seems to host at least a dozen different spirits. Those who claim to have seen ghosts standing on the very top of the light, usually gesturing out to sea, waving their arms to help ward off ships in danger, have such different descriptions of the apparitions as to suggest hauntings by many different individual ghosts.

Atlantic City boasts that at 171 feet, Absecon Lighthouse is the tallest in New Jersey. But as with many other things about the old "Queen of the Jersey Shore," this is a slight exaggeration on the part of local boosters. It's only a very slight one, however, for Barnegat Lighthouse is just a foot taller. In fact, the two lights most likely were intended to be built from exactly the same plans, as both were constructed—Absecon Light in 1857, followed by Barnegat Light in 1859—under the supervision of Army engineer George Gordon Meade, who later went on to fame as the Union general who won the Battle of Gettysburg.

Lighthouses warn sailors of particularly dangerous locations along seacoasts. They are expensive to build and maintain, so the decision to erect one comes only after a particular spot along the shore has proven to be especially dangerous—after the cape or inlet has racked up a large number of wrecks and resulted in a sufficiently impressive death toll.

The many ghosts atop Absecon Lighthouse likely represent a long list of maritime disasters that erecting the light earlier may have prevented. Among the ghosts observed at the lighthouse is a British soldier of the Revolutionary War period. His red and white uniform is spotless, his musket held at the port arms position, as if ready for inspection. The historical record shows that, sure enough, a whole boatload of British soldiers perished in a wreck off Absecon Island. On March 31, 1779, a late-spring snowstorm reduced visibility to yards rather than miles. His Majesty's troop transport *Mermaid* was en route from Halifax, Nova Scotia, to New York to reinforce British forces occupying the city. Blown off course by the raging storm, the *Mermaid* ran aground on a sandbar and broke up in the high surf. At least 145 soldiers and crew died, their corpses washed up on what is now America's Playground's beach.

So many more wrecks occurred in the vicinity that Dr. Jonathan Pitney, the "father" of Atlantic City, persuaded Congress in 1845 to appropriate $5,000 for a feasibility study of building a lighthouse there. Perhaps he should have introduced Congress to the ghosts of the many shipwreck victims. By the time it was completed more than a decade later, on January 15, 1857, the Absecon Lighthouse had cost a total of $52,187. But the cost of waiting so long was hundreds of lives.

Are the ghosts of shipwrecks past bitter? Or, as they gaze seaward from their perches atop Absecon Lighthouse, are they relieved that ships at sea now are warned of the hazards of the inlet and beach?

A Room with a View

The trouble began when the middle-aged couple moved into their dream home, a seafront condo in Brigantine. At last they could afford a beautiful apartment overlooking the ocean. The husband's family had always regarded the seashore as a very special place and their favorite vacation destination. Now the two successful professionals could live there year-round and recall the many happy family times spent on the beach.

In decorating their new condo, the husband and wife decided to hang their collection of family pictures in the foyer, where they and their guests could see them whenever entering or leaving the apartment. Their collection, beautifully mounted in antique frames, was carefully arranged and hung. The next morning, however, one picture had fallen to the floor. It was a large photograph of their dear aunt Dorothy, who had died recently. The handsomely framed studio portrait captured Dorothy's friendly, outgoing, and rather determined personality. Dorothy had always known what she liked and had been persistent in getting things her way. She was always a generous person, and it was an unexpected large bequest to the couple in Dorothy's will that had made the luxury condo purchase possible. Aunt Dorothy's picture had a place of honor among the collection of family portraits. It was rehung on the wall, this time with a sturdier hook.

But the next morning, the same picture was on the floor again. The glass had cracked but the photo was unharmed. The glass was replaced and the picture rehung, this time on two large hooks. The following morning, the portrait of Dorothy again was on the floor. The couple had heard nothing during the night, and no other picture had been disturbed.

This was getting ridiculous. This time, a sturdier frame was bolted directly into a wall stud. Dorothy surely would stay put this time. Wrong. The next morning, the solid wood frame had been wrenched from the wall, shattering the frame and glass. Dorothy's image, in perfect condition, was found about twenty feet away, in the oceanfront living room.

It was then that the couple recalled the fact that on her annual seaside vacation, Dorothy had always insisted on an oceanfront room, gladly paying the premium price for a room with a sea view. The rhythmic crash of waves on the beach, the repeated advances and retreats of the tides, the play of light on the sea all fascinated Dorothy. In life, she always wanted a room with a view. Now, in death, did she still demand to see the ocean? Enclosed in a lovely new frame, Dorothy's portrait was mounted in a new location—a living-room wall facing the windows overlooking the sea.

Ever since Aunt Dorothy has been given a fine view of the Atlantic, her picture has remained on the wall. Does her smile look a bit more smug now that she's gotten her way? It's hard to tell.

The Pinelands

The Wizard of the Pines

New Jersey's Pinelands, which lie just inland from the seashore, have hosted a number of notorious characters, including the infamous Jersey Devil himself. Some of the more interesting supernatural occurrences were associated with Jerry Munyon, known as the "Wizard of the Pines," or sometimes the "Wizard of Hanover Furnace."

Jerry, the story goes, had big ambition but a poor work ethic. He wished to live well but preferred not to have to work hard to earn his living. He liked his leisure almost as well as he liked his drink. And drink cost money. One fine day, as Jerry was relaxing under a tree, having sneaked away from his work at an iron furnace, a stranger approached. Flashing a truly wicked grin, the stranger inquired if Jerry would like to live well, with money in his pockets and a full belly, without having to work. Jerry definitely was interested. "In return for my granting you magic powers, you must agree that upon your death, your soul belongs to the Devil—namely, me," offered the stranger. "Done!" said Jerry.

When he returned to work at the furnace, his boss told Jerry that he should not expect any pay that week, as he had done little work. "Fine," said Jerry. "Look me up when you need me to restart the furnace," and the fires suddenly died. After being unable to get the fires burning again, the boss finally sent for Jerry, who offered to start the furnace for a fee. When given his money, Jerry clapped his hands. A flock of white crows that had been blocking the chimney flew out, and the furnace was back in production. And for a small weekly donation to Jerry, it continued production.

Jerry had other ways to earn money through wizardry. He could "witch" a team of horses into a pond until their owner ransomed them with a money gift. Similarly, he could send cattle wading into a swamp until he was paid to send them back home. He could turn clamshells into silver dollars, with which he paid his large bar tabs. When the wizard left the bar, however, the coins turned back into clamshells.

Once Jerry approached a neighbor and asked for food. His neighbor angrily refused to give him a handout, and then brushed by him to go to her well. When she returned, she screamed and dropped her pail, for the wizard now sat on her doorstep, holding his severed head in his lap and carefully combing his hair.

On the night of his death, there was a knock at the door, and the barely conscious wizard asked his wife to answer it. A tall, grinning stranger was asking for him. Jerry began to tremble violently. "It's the Devil," he told his wife. "He's come for my soul. Tell him I'm ready." And with that, he breathed his last.

There are those who still blame the wizard for any mischief that happens in the neighborhood. They believe that Jerry prefers roaming the woods at night to spending all his time in hell. It's best not to refuse him a free meal if he shows up at your door.

The Wreck of the Blue Comet

The Jersey Shore and railroads grew up together. From the earliest days of railroads in New Jersey up until about 1920, the trains brought far more people to the beaches than any other means of transport. There was a lot of competition among the resorts and the different railroads. Atlantic City was created by a railroad and at one time was served by three different railroads, which competed in attractive ticket prices as well as in luxury and speed—above all, speed. And speed can kill. There were some notorious train wrecks on the seashore routes as the railroads offered faster and faster express service. In 1920, of the four fastest passenger trains in the world, three carried vacationers to Atlantic City. Train wrecks, like other examples of sudden and violent death, seem to create ghosts. One of the most famous train wrecks on the way to the seashore was on the fabulous Blue Comet.

Travel through Chatsworth on a warm summer night, and you just might catch an echo of a tragedy that occurred near that small town on August 19, 1939. Some say that the ghosts of the hapless passengers who rode the Blue Comet that day still haunt the site where the high-speed luxury train derailed, resulting in the death of almost everyone on board.

The Blue Comet was a specialty train that traveled from Jersey City down through the Pine Barrens. Owned and operated by the Central Railroad of New Jersey, the train made two round-trips every day in less than three hours. It made one stop in Hammonton to pick up additional passengers before continuing on to Atlantic City. The Blue Comet was blue inside and out. The cars and sleek diesel engines were blue, as were the seats, carpeting, and table linens. The men who worked the line wore blue uniforms, and the tickets purchased for the ride were also blue.

It was an immediately popular ride after it first started its run on February 21, 1929. At that time, Atlantic City had experienced another renaissance, and gambling, liquor, and sex were available almost anywhere in that wide-open town. For ten years the train carried passengers back and forth from North Jersey to the Queen of Resorts, until that fateful day in August when the rains began to fall.

South Jersey had been experiencing a serious drought for many weeks. But on August 19, the sky turned overcast and released a torrential downpour. More than eight inches of rain fell within just a few hours. Water flooded the rail line, and when the Blue Comet hit the stretch near Chatsworth, it canted off the tracks. Brakes squealed and passengers screamed as the train slid to a stop. Local residents described the crash as horrendous, and hundreds were killed in the wreck.

Today the rusting remains of the train still lie scattered along the abandoned stretch of track, which went out of use a few years later. If you listen closely, however, you might still hear the haunting, wailing whistle that once resounded through the Pine Barrens, letting area residents know that the Blue Comet was flying by—on its final, fatal run.

The Jersey Devil Has Company

While the Jersey Devil is the most famous of all New Jersey's monsters, he seems to have developed some competition in recent years. Apparently Bigfoot, although allegedly a denizen of the West, has been sighted at least fourteen times in the Garden State, according to the Bigfoot tracking website. The reports, which come primarily from the Pine Barrens in Burlington County, range from alleged sightings to noises and footprints that were deemed characteristic of the creature.

In 1997, thirty campers participated in a three-day hike on the Batona Trail, a path that winds through the heart of the Pinelands. One restless camper reported that after they had made camp for the night, he was awakened about 1:30 in the morning "by a terrible scream" that was like nothing he had ever heard before. Later that morning, several other hikers admitted that they also had heard the noise but had been too frightened to move or say anything. Such wails and the sound of something large moving through the bushes periodically frightens campers and are believed to be signs of Bigfoot, because he frequents watering places off the beaten track.

Other regions where Bigfoot has been spotted include rural parts of Ocean County. One detailed account was offered by a woman who believed she had encountered Bigfoot on a warm summer day back in 1970. She was about nine years old at the time, visiting an uncle who lived in a wooded rural area. While walking near the stream that ran behind her uncle's house, she heard noises in the brush on the other side of the water. Although she thought at first that it was probably her older brothers, she soon observed a strange figure approaching. "It appeared to be very big and was covered completely in dark long hair. I thought maybe it was a bear but the face was not like a bear at all," the woman recalled. "It stopped in front of me and looked directly at me. . . . I closed my eyes, held my breath, and waited for it to kill me or leave. . . . Thankfully it left, just walked away."

Although many years had passed, the woman clearly recalled how terrified she had been of the startling creature. She ran back to her uncle's house, crying, and because she was so frightened, her family moved to a nearby hotel for the remainder of their visit.

Like many other ethnic groups who brought the legends of their various homelands with them to the United States, New Jersey's Puerto Rican community in recent years has shared tales of a creature known as the Chupacabra, or "Goat Sucker." Since the early 1990s, the monster reportedly has appeared in the Pine Barrens and farmlands of South Jersey, where it has attacked farm animals, dogs, and cats.

Although it is usually described as vaguely human in appearance, the Chupacabra, which emits a strong sulfuric stench, is also said to have goatlike legs and to be able to change colors like a chameleon in order to blend into its surroundings. It has fiery red eyes and fangs protruding from its slitlike mouth, usually used to bite its animal victims in the neck. Circular puncture wounds, grouped in triangular patterns, apparently cause instant death. Like the Jersey Devil, "Chupie," as it is sometimes called, reportedly has never killed a human being, but its frightening appearance has startled more than one farmer into reaching for the nearest shotgun.

The Legend of the Jersey Devil

Until about the middle of the nineteenth century, most of New Jersey's seashore was a pretty desolate place, with few towns. Only Toms River and Cape May could be considered to be thriving, if relatively small, places. Behind the lonely, windswept beaches and extensive marshes lay the famous Pine Barrens, another landscape almost empty of people.

It was in these remote and isolated seashore and Pinelands environments that the legends of the Jersey Devil were born. There are several different versions of the Jersey Devil's origins. One story puts his birthplace at Leeds Point, near the present-day Brigantine National Wildlife Refuge. In other stories, the Devil first came into this world in Pleasantville, just behind Atlantic City on the mainland, or at Estellville in nearby Cape May County. Some say that his father was Satan himself, although his mother was human.

The Jersey Devil was said to have been the thirteenth—and most unwelcome—child of either the Leeds or Shourds family. Exhausted by the pain of constant childbirth, his mother cursed the child as

he was being born. She was shocked, however, when the midwife delivered a baby that was far from human.

Over the years, the creature has been described as having the head of a horse or cow, a body like that of a kangaroo or horse, and feet like a pig's. Some describe him with the talons of an eagle, but others say he inherited his father's cloven hooves. As the legend goes, the Jersey Devil escaped from his home immediately after birth, either through an open window or up a chimney. Although some claim that the young monster's first meal consisted of his twelve older siblings, most people don't believe the Devil has ever attacked a human being.

In some versions of his story, the Jersey Devil is said to have periodically stopped to visit his mother, just to make sure that all was well with her. In his role as a good son, the Jersey Devil would bring her presents and be on his best behavior—at least until any strangers happened by, in which case the Devil would fly away.

Despite his frightening appearance and supernatural powers, the Jersey Devil apparently never has actually attacked a human. At one time he is said to have killed and eaten a rottweiler dog guarding a henhouse. The Jersey Devil seems to have a big appetite for chickens and will also eat pigs, goats, sheep, and raccoons. When chickens and other farm animals go missing in the night, farmers report strange tracks nearby that look as if they were made by the hooves of a large goat.

New Jersey's own Devil first was mentioned in writing in 1735, and it is known that a Daniel Leeds homestead was at Leeds Point, near the Great Egg Harbor. Mrs. Leeds usually is credited, if that is the word, with giving birth to the Devil that year. If the Jersey Devil did make his appearance in 1735, he is more than 270 years old.

In the early nineteenth century, the Jersey Devil made a memorable visit to Cape May. It seems that a naval hero who visited Cape May often, Commodore Stephen Decatur, had been assigned to test weapons for the Army and Navy. He was test-firing artillery on an isolated beach when a strange creature flew across the sky. Decatur fired at it and hit it, but the weird apparition just flew on, out of sight. Rattled, the commodore reported his experience to the townspeople. "Oh, that's just the Jersey Devil," they assured him.

A far older version of the Devil's origins dates to the Lenni-Lenape, a local tribe whose traditions included a mysterious "night monster" that would appear on occasion to terrify villagers and frighten away game animals. Children were told never to venture into the woods after dark, because the night monster might catch and eat them. The more common story, however, is that the Jersey Devil was the child of a European immigrant who arrived in New Jersey in the eighteenth century.

The first published account of the Jersey Devil, titled "In the Pines" in the *Atlantic Monthly* in 1859, stated that the child was born human, but "no sooner did he see the light than he assumed the form of a fiend, with a horse's head, wings of a bat, and a serpent's tail." Since that time, his activities have been recorded in newspapers, periodicals, and folktales. The Devil reportedly has been seen throughout South Jersey, from Pleasantville to Philadelphia, Cape May, and many points in between. Some claim that he usually appears whenever the threat of war is in the air. In the mid-1970s, it was even claimed that he had been seen in Texas, although most New Jersey residents doubt that the creature would have strayed that far from home. In 1939, a New Jersey guidebook listed the Phantom of the Pines as the official "state demon." The 1976 book *The Jersey Devil,* by James F. McCloy and Ray Miller Jr., has remained so popular that it is now in its fifteenth printing. In 2001, the first full-length film about the Jersey Devil, titled *13th Child: The Legend of the Jersey Devil,* was released. Unfortunately, it completely lost sight of the original myth and became just another horror movie.

Thanks to all this public attention, the Jersey Devil has lived a long and healthy life and is the best-known New Jersey myth. One of the primary reasons he has stuck around so long may be because he apparently helped keep outsiders from uncovering some of the secrets that lay hidden within the Pine Barrens. During the Revolutionary War, he may have kept British troops from investigating any suspicious lights or noises that they saw in the night. It is said that the locals, tired of his mischief, hired an itinerant preacher to exorcise the Jersey Devil, who was cast out of the woods for one hundred years. When he returned, the Devil reportedly wreaked havoc for weeks, as though punishing Pinelands residents for what he perceived as their betrayal.

The Jersey Devil is most likely to frighten the wits out of people on moonless nights in the areas where coastal marshes border on pine woods. His eyes glow red in the dark as he stalks his human prey—only to put a good scare into them before flying off. It must be said that many of those who have encountered the monster have had more than a few drinks. One theory is that the Jersey Devil actually is in the pay of teetotaler prohibitionists who wish to scare drunks into sobriety. Some who have met the Jersey Devil are said to have stopped drinking for entire weeks.

The Bottomless "Blue Hole"

Why do some places feel more mysterious than others? What causes them to resonate with a certain level of energy that parapsychologists term "supernatural"? Whatever the reasons, the myths and legends that have sprung up about such locations have been handed down to this day through the generations.

One such unique spot is the mysterious Blue Hole near the tiny town of Winslow, close to the Great Egg Harbor River. Not readily accessible, the Blue Hole is on private property; do not trespass. The crystalline waters are frigid but completely clear because no vegetation grows within the pool. It was named the Blue Hole because its transparent waters reflect the color of the sky. Supposedly, springs of medicinal value form a whirlpool at the center of the hole and drain downward toward the Atlantic Ocean. Scientists who have tried to measure the depth of the Blue Hole apparently have been stymied by the fact that their lines never seemed to reach the bottom, a fact that supported the "bottomless pit" theory.

Although the region has been populated since the mid-eighteenth century, no settlement has imposed upon the serenity that surrounds the Blue Hole, which continues to fascinate visitors because of its untamed quality. Stories have been told of beautiful young women being drawn below the surface, where they lie through eternity in "submarine splendor." Young men have also reported being seized by unseen hands that tried to drag them down. A Native American tale says that the Blue Hole was born from the tears of a maiden crying over her faithless lover. But to this day, nothing has explained the presence of a crystal blue lake in a region best known for its tea-colored, cedar-fed waterways and nearby salty, green ocean

Science doesn't have an answer, but does the solution lie in the realm of the supernatural? The few fishermen brave enough to drop a line into the Blue Hole report that they've never caught a fish there, nor even seen one in the hole. But their bait always disappears from their hooks, and some say that afterward the hooks look polished and shiny, even if they started into the Blue Hole rusty or tarnished. Who or what took the bait without getting caught? Perhaps we don't want to know.

Are Ghost Sightings a Symptom of "Apple Palsy"?

Skeptics like to think that the high frequency of supernatural encounters reported in the Pinelands near the seashore is related to the abundance of illegal stills in the sparsely settled woods. Moonshining has been a common activity there for centuries and is said to continue to this day. "Jersey lightning," "crackskull" (referring to the subsequent hangover), "applejack," and just plain "jack" all describe the favorite product of Pineland moonshiners, who take pride in the alcohol content of their product. In the late nineteenth century, it was estimated that there was one still for every thousand people living in the Pines. When locals saw a person trembling or staggering under the influence, that person was said to be suffering from "apple palsy."

There is a story that a city fellow once asked to buy some jack. "We have two kinds," replied the moonshiner. "Which do you want?" "What's the difference?" asked the outsider. "You going fighting or courting?" was the rejoinder. Maybe there is a third kind—the drink that will cause visions of ghosts.

Ghost Towns of the Pinelands

Forget the mental image of ghost towns of the Old West—picturesque, largely intact buildings preserved in remote deserts and high mountains. The New Jersey Pinelands' ghost towns have suffered a longer period of neglect than most western ghost towns. Vandals, forest fires, and souvenir hunters all have taken their toll on them. In South Jersey today, only the ghosts are left, along with the Jersey Devil and some other mysterious phenomena.

For the same reason that the more famous ghost towns of the West came to be, South Jersey has many ghost towns, which often have resident ghosts. Ghost towns are abandoned, at least by their living residents, because their economic base disappears, as so often happens when a mine is exhausted.

How can New Jersey, statistically the most crowded state in the Union, have ghost towns? The changing fortunes of the iron industry in the Pinelands explain most of the abandoned communities that make South Jersey the eastern United States' ghost town capital.

Imagine the plight of the South Jersey ironworkers. In the Colonial period, and especially during the Revolution, their products were much in demand. Their cannons and cannonballs were vital in winning America's freedom. In the first half of the nineteenth century, New Jersey was the third most important iron-producing state. In the Southern Pines, once-thriving iron centers such as Weymouth, Atsion, Hampton Furnace, Mary Ann Furnace, Batsto, and Martha's Furnace are now all but gone. Through no fault of their own, as their products were acknowledged to be of high quality, the ironmasters were forced out of business by events far away and beyond their control. Pennsylvania coal, Great Lakes iron ores, new technologies—all of these things led to the death of the once bustling little communities as surely as the fires died out in the furnaces.

And so ghosts abound in the Pinelands, where lonely pine forests help hide the ghost towns and their many ghosts and legendary monsters and witches—only a few miles from crowded seashore resorts.

The Dancing Bandit

In times past, the lonely roads across the Pinelands held more danger than just getting stuck in the loose sand. Highwaymen roamed the narrow, old roads through the dense woods, accosting lone travelers with a gun and the demand "Stand and deliver!" And deliver they would, for this was a case of their money or their life.

The most famous of the early highwaymen was Joe Mulliner, who was active in the 1770s and 1780s, when deserters from both the American and British Armies hid out in the woods and made a living off robberies, smuggling, extortion, and moonshining. Highwaymen like Joe Mulliner not only robbed travelers, but also extorted "protection money" from local citizens to leave them alone. Tavern owners in particular paid highwaymen not to rob their guests, at least until the guests had paid their bills for lodging, food, and drink. Joe was unique in that he robbed only the rich. If a poor traveler, ordered to stand and deliver, could deliver but a few coins, Joe usually let him keep his money and sent him on his way. Joe also gave money to the poorest of his neighbors, saying it was truly a crime to let a fellow human starve. His generosity to the poor and to church poor boxes made Joe Mulliner a local hero—a sort of homegrown Robin Hood.

Joe is said to have been a Tory, an American who remained loyal to the king during the American Revolution. Whatever his politics, he led a band of as many as a hundred loyalists during the war. Under the pretense of attacking patriots as enemies of the Crown, he may have been just looking for an excuse to rob and harass his neighbors. Joe was aware of his Robin Hood image and worked to polish it, hoping to earn the respect of people to the point where they wouldn't betray his whereabouts to the authorities. For example, when the Widow Bates returned from church one Sunday to find Mulliner's gang, but not Joe himself, plundering her house, she protested loudly. She "cussed them out" so vigorously that the thugs tied her to a tree and burned down her house in front of her. This was bad public relations, to say the least. It is said that Joe Mulliner, realizing that his men had crossed the line into outrageous violence, anonymously sent the widow $300 as an apology.

Joe was said to have taken a fancy to Honore Read, the beautiful daughter of the ironmaster who lived at Pleasant Mills, near Batsto. Honore knew of Joe's fascination with her, but her rich father was not at all pleased about the charming—and married—outlaw's intentions. When Honore was to be the hostess of a great party to celebrate her birthday, the guest list was quite long, but it did not include Joe Mulliner, who definitely expected an invitation. There are two versions of what happened next. According to one source, Joe defiantly crashed the party and danced with Honore in a whirling dance that gave frustrated onlookers no chance to grab him without endangering his partner. Finally, Joe whirled Honore right out the door, using her as a temporary hostage, then leaped upon his horse and disappeared.

In the second version, Joe kidnapped Honore from her house on the afternoon of the party. Her ransom, as the story went, was his demand of Honore that she, in the delicate language of the day, give him her "wholehearted affection." Whatever took place, Honore returned safely on time for her party. Neither Joe nor Honore would ever say what persuaded him to let her go free.

Joe was soon afterward captured by a vigilante posse one night at a tavern, which still stands in the tiny rural town of Nesco. Arrowhead Tavern, known today as Indian Cabin Tavern, is distinguished by a small historical marker that states, "Joseph Mulliner noted refugee—Tory—outlaw captured here in 1781."

Mulliner was tried and sentenced to hang in Burlington, West Jersey's capital at the time, supposedly as an example of the fate that awaited other "gentlemen of the road." According to Henry C. Beck in *Forgotten Towns of Southern New Jersey,* the highwayman was probably "strung up officially at Woodbury gaol," like others before him.

In the 1960s, some local pranksters set up a tombstone in Pleasant Mills that supposedly marked the site of Mulliner's grave. It is more than likely, however, that his body was laid to rest on land along the Mullica River that was owned by his wife. But his spirit does not rest. "Stand and deliver!" shouts the ghost that some claim to have met on dark nights. At other times, the ghost of Joe Mulliner can be seen spinning his sweetheart about merrily as he dances to ghostly music.

Fiddling with the Devil

Legends have always followed gifted musicians, some of whom reportedly were willing to "sell their souls" for the opportunity to play the perfect song or sing the perfect note. Others have allegedly challenged the Devil in musical contests in order to save their souls—or possibly just to satisfy their egos and prove they were more talented than the Prince of Darkness.

One such fiddler, renowned throughout the Pinelands for his playing, was Sammy Giberson, sometimes known as Sammy Buck, who was repeatedly heard to declare he could outplay the Devil himself. It was unlikely that Sammy ever expected anyone to accept his challenge. Still, he was not too surprised when, on his way home from a local dance one night, he was confronted at a bridge by a tall, dark stranger who proved to be none other than Satan.

Residents of the Pinelands still delight in telling of the duel between Sammy and the Devil, as they drew their bows and began to play. For every song that Satan selected, Sammy offered an equally difficult tune, until finally he began a song so sweet, so mournful, and so intricate that the Devil was unable to continue. Fortunately for Sammy, Old Nick was so moved by the music that he was a gracious loser. And Sammy Giberson continued on his way home, knowing that he had not boasted about his talent in vain.

In another version of the story, Sammy was drunk on moonshine when Satan challenged him to a musical duel. Many neighbors heard two fiddles playing on that dark night. Supposedly Sammy, tiring in this fast and furious bout of fiddling, slipped in a hymn, which forced the Devil to withdraw and disappear, handing Sammy the victory by default.

After Sammy died, the fiddle was locked away in a box, but it still played by itself on occasion. On dark, moonless nights, the local people can hear a fiddle playing achingly sweet music. Is it Sammy or the Devil playing? No one knows for sure.

Although there are other versions in which Sammy loses and forfeits his soul, most people who relate the tale prefer to have him finish as the winner.

Northern Tidewater

The Ghost of the Traitor General

A most unusual ghost has been observed stalking the Navesink Highlands, peering anxiously out to sea. Is he looking for the British fleet that he thinks will enable the final defeat of the Revolutionaries and keep America in the British Empire?

The slender, almost emaciated ghost wears the uniform of an American Revolutionary War officer, but without its brass buttons or insignia. This officer had been court-martialed, stripped of his rank as general, and was strongly suspected of treason. He stands atop the Highlands looking in vain for his friends and true employers, the British.

This is the ghost of General Charles Lee, the man who tried to betray the patriots' cause in the Revolution, the despised aristocrat whose spirit cannot now rest in American soil. Lee was born in 1731, the son of a British general, and joined the British Army at age eleven. He earned a reputation as a valiant soldier fighting in the French and Indian War. When America declared its independence, Lee resigned his commission in the British Army, and because he was an experienced officer, he was made a general in the American Army, second in rank to Washington himself. He hated the man and gave Washington plenty of reasons to hate him.

Treacherously indecisive, Lee was supposed to support Washington's attack on Trenton at Christmas 1776 but failed to show up in time to help. Washington won anyway but began to wonder just whose side Lee was on.

In 1778, British general Henry Clinton decided to abandon Philadelphia and march across New Jersey to New York. George Washington decided to attack the British as they retreated, partly in order to capture badly needed ammunition, guns, and supplies from the twelve-mile-long line of baggage wagons trailing after Clinton's troops.

Lee at first refused an opportunity to command troops in support of Washington's force attacking at Monmouth, then changed his mind. He was supposed to coordinate his attack with Washington's but retreated instead of attacking when he should have. Just as at Trenton, Washington won the battle despite Lee's fumbling. After the battle, witnesses claim that Washington angrily used every known curse word, and probably invented some, in publicly and personally relieving Lee of command. Lee was court-martialed on July 4 and never again went into battle.

Washington strongly suspected that Lee was a spy, still loyal to the king, but couldn't prove it. Years later, in 1855, a document was found in Lee's handwriting laying out a plan for the British to win the war. He was a traitor after all, and his spirit is condemned to wander, looking in vain for his British friends to sail into Sandy Hook Bay.

The Ghost of Mary Rogers

Believe it or not, Hoboken's riverfront was once a popular resort. In the first half of the nineteenth century, it had a tree-shaded "riverwalk" lined with taverns and beer gardens. And it was on a Hoboken waterfront recreation area, Elysian Fields, that the first-ever baseball game was played. But the early resort for stressed New Yorkers was the site of a brutal murder that became the most famous crime of the times.

The ghost of the beautiful young woman whose body was found floating in the Hudson River just offshore still haunts the waterfront. The corpse of Mary Cecelia Rogers was found on July 28, 1841. She had been missing from her New York City home for three days. Mary had been sexually abused and beaten to death. Had she been lured to the romantic riverwalk by a lover who then raped and murdered her?

The lovely twenty-year-old girl had sold newspapers at a stand near the offices of several popular New York newspapers. All the reporters had known her, and they made her rape-murder into a sensational story, the 1841 equivalent of the O. J. Simpson case. Had she been kidnapped by a man or a group of men? Had one of her many lovers gotten a little carried away during rough sex? One of her boyfriends, Donald Payne, was arrested, questioned, and eventually released. He committed suicide on the Hoboken shore, near where Mary's body had been discovered. A year later, a Hoboken innkeeper, in a deathbed confession, claimed that Mary Rogers had come to the town for an abortion. The operation was butchered, and the doctor and innkeeper had brutalized her body to make it look like a crime of passion. But many doubted this story.

A then unknown writer living in Hoboken at the time wrote a fictional version of Mary Rogers's murder, changing the locale to Paris and calling her Marie Roget. *The Mystery of Marie Roget* has been called the first modern mystery story and helped make Edgar Allan Poe famous.

To this day, the case remains officially unsolved. And the ghost of Mary Rogers still haunts the riverfront.

The Ghost of Washington's Spy

Standing atop the Navesink Highlands, staring out at Sandy Hook and, in the distance, New York Bay, the ghost of Washington's spy has been spotted watching for the British fleet to finally evacuate New York. The Revolutionary War was over at last, won by the efforts of patriots like John Honeyman, George Washington's most effective spy. His is an interesting story.

Honeyman was born in Armagh, Ireland, in 1729. Drafted into the British Army, he once saved General James Wolfe's life in a shipboard accident. The grateful general made John his adjutant, but Honeyman could not prevent Wolfe's death in action at the Battle of Quebec.

Discharged from the British Army, Honeyman met General Washington at Fort Lee and agreed to act as a spy. Honeyman pretended to be a loyalist, selling cattle and horses to the British forces. His information about British troop strength, location, and supplies helped Washington win at Trenton. Washington told his troops that Honeyman was a traitor to the American cause and, if captured, must be brought alive to Washington for questioning. This happened, and General Washington then helped him "escape" unharmed to resume his spying.

Once a mob of patriots was about to burn down Honeyman's house to punish the "traitor," but his wife was able to show them a letter from Washington himself testifying to Honeyman's service to the American Army.

Honeyman's last assignment? "Let me know when the British fleet leaves New York," said Washington, and his spy is still on alert for British military movements.

Jimmy Hoffa's Ghost Cheers Them On

In life, people either loved or hated Jimmy Hoffa. To many in the rank and file of the Teamsters Union, James R. Hoffa was a hero— a former truck driver who became a fearless labor organizer, a man who fought hard to negotiate decent wages and pensions for hard-working union members. To others, he was a corrupt associate of organized crime figures.

Pardoned from prison by President Richard Nixon, Jimmy Hoffa disappeared permanently and mysteriously in 1975. It was widely assumed but never proven that he was kidnapped and murdered by the Mob. His body has never been found. But in a magazine interview, onetime mobster Donald "Tony the Greek" Frankos, then in the Federal Witness Protection Program, alleged that Jimmy's body had been secretly dumped into a foundation for concrete supports at Giants (Meadowland) Stadium, then under construction, on the banks of the Berry Creek Canal, which joins the Hackensack River just above Newark Bay. The exact site is said to be under section 107, just off the corner of the western end zone.

Although in life Hoffa was known to hold a grudge, his ghost apparently has decided to relax and enjoy his permanent season ticket. Fans, players, and maintenance crew members alike have reported ghostly cheers coming from beneath the stands at the location. Though Jimmy Hoffa was believed to be a Detroit Lions fan, his ghost seems to cheer for any good, aggressive play, regardless of the team. A few players even swear they've heard some unduly harsh criticism from deep beneath the stands if they fumble an easy one.

The Triple Airship Still Flies

Seeing something inexplicable up in the sky has been an experience shared by many. Just what is it that people have seen when they report something very strange in the heavens? Consider some of the explanations offered by those who disbelieve sightings of UFOs: Were the phenomena simply lights reflected by cloud formations—lights originating on the ground or those of conventional aircraft? Were they mirages caused by light refracted by air currents? Were they ordinary high-altitude weather balloons, although such balloons haven't been used now for decades? Or could they possibly have been the ghosts of airplanes, airships, or balloons long gone?

A few thoroughly puzzled observers think they've briefly seen a unique object dodging in and out of the clouds over Raritan and Sandy Hook Bays. Quite unlike the giant airships or dirigibles that long ago landed at Lakehurst, such as the doomed Hindenburg, this weird contraption is said to look like three cigar-shaped balloons tied together horizontally.

As odd as that sounds, it describes a curious early attempt at an airship that actually did fly over these waters once. Dr. Solomon Andrews of Perth Amboy was the world's greatest inventor. He'd tell people that himself, often and loudly. The term "crackpot" could have been coined to describe him. He was a physician who just loved to tinker with new ideas. He did have a proven success: He invented an "unpickable" padlock. Thieves eventually did figure out how to pick it open, but still, it was a tough lock. It made Dr. Andrews a small fortune, which he proceeded to spend developing a kind of early blimp, which he called an "aereon." The three connected cylindrical gasbags were filled with hydrogen. The good doctor claimed that he could actually steer his aereon, navigating the air like a ship navigates the seas. How did he control its speed, height, and direction without having an engine of any kind? Well that's a secret. A big secret. No one else ever discovered it.

We do know that it did fly on several occasions—many people saw it. When the Civil War started, Dr. Andrews tried to persuade the Union to buy his designs to build observation airships to spy on Confederate troops. He even got an interview with President Lincoln. But he never got a government contract. After the war, he tried to raise money to build a huge aereon to carry passengers between New York and Philadelphia, but the project never got off the ground, so to speak.

To the end of his life, the eccentric and secretive inventor built a series of experimental airships, determined to prove his ideas. Perhaps his persistence has propelled his "maneuverable balloon" ideas forward into the spirit world.

The Poetic Ghost from Matawan

Folks in the vicinity of Keyport and Union Beach on Raritan Bay say that they've witnessed a strange sight: A figure dressed in the uniform of a New Jersey militiaman of the Revolutionary War patrols the coast, observing shipping in the bay. At his heels walks a little dog. If approached, both man and dog evaporate like a morning fog. Who could this be? Or, more accurately, whose ghost is this?

The more history-minded ghost hunters believe that Philip Freneau, the "poet of the Revolution," is still on patrol, carrying out his wartime mission of keeping an eye on shipping. Freneau was a spy for the patriotic cause and a passionate advocate of freedom.

Freneau's place in history now rests upon his literary efforts, but he wore many hats in his life. He was born to French emigrant parents in what was then called Middletown Point, now Matawan. He was both a sea captain and merchant, often sailing to the Portuguese Island of Madeira to buy their famous wines for his thirsty customers. Freneau also was familiar with the Caribbean Islands, where he dealt in rum.

When his liquor and wine import business was wiped out by the British blockade during the Revolutionary War, Philip became very active in the American cause. His writings strongly supported the war, and his role as a spy and coastguardsman landed him in trouble. He patrolled the bayshores with his little dog, Sancho. Sancho's barks would alert Freneau if any American loyalists were spying on the spy. Eventually, Freneau's luck ran out. He was on an American ship that tried to run the British blockage but was captured. Freneau did time in British military prisons, an experience that deepened his hatred of the British and made his poetry even more vehemently in favor of violence against the enemy.

If he were alive today, Philip Freneau would be termed a "hawk" for his attitude toward war. In his mind, war was justified by the need to overthrow monarchies wherever they existed. When the French Revolution broke out, Freneau was all in favor of joining the French in attacking Britain and accused President George Washington of being a timid pacifist in staying out of the struggle. Washington, in turn, publicly labeled Freneau a "damned rascal."

Some claim that the ghost of Philip Freneau, together with that of his dog Sancho, makes more frequent appearances when America is at war. Don't approach the ghostly man and dog, though. Sancho is every bit as aggressive as his master.

Delaware

Bay and River

The Town Named for a Disaster

Mauricetown, a charming little town on the lower Maurice River near Delaware Bay, was once an important Colonial port, home to sailors and fishermen. Oddly, for a sailors' home and refuge, the town and river were named for a maritime disaster.

Early in the Colonial period, it seems that a ship called the *Prince Maurice* was captured by hostile Indians. The sailing vessel had slowed to navigate a tight bend in the little river, when Indians leaped aboard and murdered the entire crew, then set the *Prince Maurice* on fire and destroyed her.

For decades afterward, sailors on ships sailing to or from Mauricetown reported that phantom canoes of warlike Indians would appear at the notorious tight bend, where ships always slowed to a crawl. That treacherous bend is still known by its Colonial name—No Man's Friend.

Stretch Garrison Rides Again

Folks living near the lower Maurice River, from the Delaware Bay to Mauricetown, recall seeing this legendary apparition out on the river, even in broad daylight. A tall, slender man, dressed in rather old-fashioned farmer's overalls, flashes by, heaving and bouncing like a rodeo cowboy riding a bull. Except that the man is not riding a bull up the river. He's riding a shark bareback and waving his big straw hat, and he's having a wonderful time. It is the spirit of the legendary "Stretch" Garrison. Nicknamed for his tall tales, which seemed to stretch the truth, Stretch was South Jersey's version of Paul Bunyan.

Everything about Stretch Garrison was wildly exaggerated. Like the story of his rooster, Big Boy. Big Boy was so tall, it was reported, that he ate his corn off the barn roof. One time, Stretch decided to go into the venison business, so he captured and trained lovely young does to seduce bucks and lure them into his slaughterhouse.

But the favorite stories about Stretch revolve around sharks. It seems that Stretch liked to lasso them and ride them on the river like wild broncos. In some stories, he tamed a shark to pull his plow across the field and the farm wagon to market.

So the next time you see a cowboy riding a shark, relax. It's just Stretch Garrison having a little fun.

Blood Money

The phrase "blood money" commonly refers to money obtained through criminal violence. Murder for hire would be a good example. There is an old legend from the banks of the Delaware River in South Jersey of blood money in both the symbolic and literal senses.

The story has it that in 1682, one Mark Newbie obtained a bank charter from the lords proprietors of West Jersey. He was able to prove that he had the capital necessary to operate a bank by displaying sacks and sacks of farthings and halfpence. The coins had been struck in Ireland to commemorate a famous massacre of Protestants by Roman Catholics. One side showed a profile of St. Patrick, Ireland's patron saint, so the coins were known as "Patrick's pence." Because the coins apparently celebrated mass murder, they were very unpopular and soon withdrawn from circulation in Protestant England.

Newbie bought them up to use in the American colonies, where they were still accepted as legal tender. There was a problem, however. Whoever handled the coins reported that they seemed to leave bloodstains on their hands. Soon, no one would touch the tainted coins. Newbie's bank went out of business, and the coins soon disappeared. No one wants blood money.

The Confederate Ghosts of Finn's Point

They volunteered to fight for their homeland, and they fought valiantly on one of the bloodiest battlefields on the continent. They survived that bloodbath, only to die ignobly of disease, malnutrition, and neglect while imprisoned in a notorious death camp. They are the Confederate dead of Finn's Point, and they are bitter and vengeful. And they march on foggy nights.

How did more than twenty-seven hundred Confederate soldiers, many of them captured at the Battle of Gettysburg, end up buried in the national cemetery at Fort Mott, in Finn's Point, New Jersey? It is a horrific story of epidemic disease, insufficient medicine, and, some say, a ruthless government policy aimed at shortening and winning the Civil War.

Finn's Point is located at a strategic point on the Delaware River, downstream from Wilmington, Delaware. Here the river has an elbow-shaped bend, where ships inbound for Philadelphia and other river ports must negotiate a forty-five-degree turn and navigate between either the Delaware or Jersey shore and Pea Patch Island, lying in the middle of the channel. Ships, especially sailing ships, must slow down as they make the turn and navigate between the little island and the New Jersey riverbank. As long ago as 1660, the Swedes built a fort at Finn's Point, named after the Finns who made up most of the population of New Sweden. Sweden ruled Finland at the time.

Pea Patch Island, as the story goes, got its name when a boat loaded with peas ran aground on a mudflat just barely above water level. The peas sprouted and grew all over the mudflat. The vines helped trap more sediment, and thus an eighty-six-acre island eventually was created.

Before the Civil War, it was decided to build new fortifications to defend Philadelphia against attack by enemy ships sailing up the Delaware. Fort Mott was built at Finn's Point, and Fort Delaware was built opposite on Pea Patch Island. The island is so swampy and low-lying that the great brick fort had to be constructed atop six thousand tree trunks driven down into the mud. Fort Delaware cost $1 million and never fired a shot. No enemy ships ever got as far as Fort Delaware or Fort Mott, because the Confederate Navy never got north of Chesapeake Bay. But Fort Delaware, out in the middle of the river, made an ideal high-security prison for captured Confederates.

There were a lot of prisoners of war on both sides during the Civil War. The South repeatedly suggested that these prisoners be exchanged, one for one. Many on the Northern side of the conflict thought that such exchanges should be made, as conditions in Confederate prison camps housing Union soldiers were terrible. The death rate at Georgia's infamous Andersonville Prison was so horrific that at war's end, the camp's superintendent was hanged for inhumane treatment.

Sadly, Fort Delaware became the Union's counterpart of Andersonville. It was hell for its prisoners. The only water supply was polluted river water. Clouds of mosquitoes bred in the swampy surroundings. Malaria and dysentery, fatal at the time, killed thousands. Daily, boatloads of corpses were ferried over to Fort Mott to be unceremoniously dumped into long trenches in Finn's Point National Cemetery next door.

President Lincoln was strongly opposed to any large-scale prisoner exchanges, although he was well aware of the horrendous death rates among both Confederate and Union prisoners of war. He also knew that the Union held a definite advantage in population size. He reasoned that one-for-one exchanges would proportionately benefit the South more than the North. Fewer Southern soldiers in the field would shorten the war and thus save more lives in the long run.

But this was small consolation to the prisoners on both sides, who no doubt considered Lincoln's policy to be devastatingly cruel. The thousands of unmarked graves at Finn's Point are testimony to the bitterness of the Civil War.

It is believed that the justifiably angry spirits of the Confederate prisoners are restless and vengeful, and now haunt Fort Delaware, Fort Mott, and Finn's Point. Many visitors have reported seeing shadowy ranks of soldiers on parade on moonless, foggy nights. The faint, poignant notes of taps are played by phantom buglers.

Two encounters with the Confederate ghosts stand out. On one occasion, tourists sightseeing at Fort Mott were delighted to see a formation of soldiers in Civil War Confederate uniforms drilling on the field. With flags flying and music playing, they marched past the tourists, never breaking their role-playing, never acknowledging the group of onlookers. Thrilled, the tourists snapped pictures. On their way out of the state park, they paused to thank the park superintendent for the colorful reenactment they'd witnessed. "Reenactment? There is no reenactment today," asserted the superintendent. None of the photographs developed later showed any soldiers.

In another case, a family out for an evening drive near the Confederate gravesites experienced a frightening car problem. Their brand new car stopped dead and would not start. Nothing electrical functioned. They had to abandon the car and walk back to the highway, terrified by a chorus of moans and shouts from the adjacent graveyard. Prominent on the car's hood were shiny chrome letters that spelled out "L-I-N-C-O-L-N."

The Youngest Confederate Ghost

Understandably, the Confederate prisoners of war held at Fort Delaware desperately tried to escape. More than three hundred prisoners made the attempt. Confederate general James Archer, captured at Gettysburg with many of his men, tried to organize a mass uprising to take over the fort and commandeer boats for an escape, but failed. He died in solitary confinement in a dark, dank cell. His last words were that the only way off Pea Patch Island was in a coffin.

One drummer boy prisoner took this advice literally. In the Civil War, it was common for boys as young as twelve or thirteen to enlist as drummer boys and messengers. The young drummer boy decided to escape in a coffin, faking his own death by chalking his face dead white and holding his breath when examined briefly by an overworked Army doctor. Other prisoners, assigned to grave-digging detail at Fort Mott's cemetery, were in on the plot and would secretly free him before burying the empty coffin he left.

Unfortunately, those particular prisoners were assigned elsewhere on the critical day, and the drummer boy was buried alive.

He died a horrible, slow death of suffocation. His ghost, still clawing at his throat as he struggles for air, now roams the graveyard, having finally escaped from his coffin.

Thar She Blows, There She Goes

The ghost of Town Bank is an unusual sight, even among ghosts. For the ghost seems to be walking on water, as she paces over what was once dry land that is now underwater.

The ghost is that of a middle-aged woman in Colonial-era apron and floor-length dress. She is one of the oldest ghosts on the Jersey coast, and as she walks along a shoreline that no longer exists, she looks out over the bay, searching not only for whales, but also for the town in which she once lived.

Although Town Bank still is a place name on Delaware Bay just north of Cape May, the original town of that name, founded in 1685, disappeared long ago under the encroaching waves. Town Bank was established by a community of whalers from New England, attracted by the many whales that once populated Delaware Bay. Hannah Gorham, a granddaughter of a Mayflower pilgrim, became famous as a whale spotter. Her sharp eyes could distinguish the small jet of vapor spouted by a whale surfacing to breathe. "Thar she blows!" was the traditional alarm shouted to the boat crew, who would quickly launch a whaleboat in pursuit.

Centuries later, Hannah still patrols the ghostly, long-eroded banks of the bay, searching for the telltale blows of the whales. Of course, Hannah is not really there. For that matter, neither is the town nor the whales.

The Hanged Pirate

Many a place along New Jersey's coast has a pirate tale to tell. New Jersey seems to have been a popular pirate hangout, especially before and during the Revolutionary War. Down in Salem County at Sharptown, along Salem Creek not far from Delaware Bay, stands an old tavern called the Seven Stars. Supposedly, the name originated when an old drunk, lying in a late-night stupor on the barroom floor, claimed that the roof over his head had such a large hole in it that he could see seven stars through it.

At any rate, the Seven Stars is said to be haunted by the ghost of a pirate who was brought to swift justice at the tavern. This pirate, known as Bluebeard, not to be confused with Blackbeard (Edward Teach), was captured while enjoying a few hearty drinks at the bar. He drunkenly admitted his guilt and promptly was hanged from an attic window. Many patrons of the Seven Stars swear they've seen Bluebeard's ghost, swinging by the neck, dangling from that attic window. Of course, having a few drinks might increase one's likelihood of spotting old Bluebeard.

The Doomed Ferryboat

The night sky over the Delaware River between Camden, New Jersey, and Philadelphia glows orange as a catastrophic fire destroys a river ferry in midstream. The swift and terrible conflagration that overwhelmed the old side-wheeler *New Jersey* took sixty-one lives, making it one of the worst boat accidents of the time.

It happened on March 15, 1856, but according to local legend, the flames can be seen, and the pitiful screaming heard, every year since on the anniversary of the disaster. Camden and Philadelphia residents living near the river have good reason to dread the ides of March, for the ghosts of the *New Jersey*'s victims still relive their last moments of death by fire or drowning.

The "Big Tub" in the Little Tub

There is an old story told about a bizarre ghost seen out on the Delaware River near the site of Fort Elfsborg, a Colonial Swedish fort in what is now Salem County, New Jersey. Though rarely seen these days, the odd sight amused locals for years in the past.

A very obese man, rowing a small rowboat out in the shipping channel, is visibly angry and upset, waving his arm about in excited, threatening gestures. This apparition could only be the ghost of the onetime governor of New Sweden, Johann Printz.

The governor was a big man. He weighed more than four hundred pounds and stood over six feet tall. His bad temper was every bit as big as his waistline, and his vocabulary of curses and obscenities was unmatched in the colonies. The Indians called him "Big Tub." Behind his back, his own colonists probably called him worse, for he ruled by fear and loathing. Fear was just about the governor's only weapon, as Sweden never really supported its far-off colony on the Delaware. Swedish Fort Elfsborg was quickly abandoned when the Dutch decided to take over New Sweden. The Dutch fleet sailed up the Delaware River in June 1651. The Swedes didn't have the men or guns to resist, so the Dutch warships simply fired blanks from their great cannons to convince the Swedes that resistance was suicidal. "Big Tub" was so angry that he set out in the rowboat to follow the Dutch ships and treat them to his most colorful curses. It must have been funny, and it certainly was ineffectual.

And so for many years afterward, the fattest and most abusive ghost the river has ever seen rowed his boat while gesturing threateningly at his unseen Dutch enemies. Just as well that we can't hear what he is shouting.

Ghostly Perfumed Smoke

It happens just before Christmas every year. Some people in the neighborhood of Greenwich, a tiny village on the banks of the Cohansey River near Delaware Bay, detect an odd smell in the damp air as fog rolls in from the bay. It is a sweet, spicy aroma—not unpleasant, but certainly unfamiliar. Could it be the ghostly smell, somehow re-created supernaturally, of burning tea?

Little Greenwich's glorious moment in history occurred on the evening of December 22, 1774. For on that cold winter night, the sky was lit by the flames of a huge bonfire on the "Greate" (Main) Street of the little river port. An entire ship's cargo of tea was burned in protest of the infamous English tax on tea. While at Boston's more famous tea party, the tea was dumped overboard into the harbor, Greenwich's patriots chose to set it on fire.

Many people say that they've seen ghosts, and many claim to have heard them. If eyes and ears can sense the supernatural, what about the nose? Actually, it's not uncommon for people to report ghostly fragrances in the air. Some report occasionally smelling a familiar odor that reminds them of a deceased loved one—a favorite perfume perhaps, or fresh baked goods, or a particular brand of pipe tobacco—when there is no known source of the aroma, except in their memories of the departed. And so the scent of all that tea, burned centuries before, perhaps reappears as an annual reminder of an act of patriotic vandalism.

The Americans who torched the tea got away with it. The story goes that the English ship *Greyhound,* loaded with the best tea from India, was bound for Philadelphia. Warned, however, of the rebels' plans to seize his cargo at Philadelphia, the captain steered into the Colonial port of Greenwich (still pronounced locally as "Green-witch"). There the tea was unloaded and stored in the cellar of a local loyalist. But word got out, and about forty patriots, disguised as Indians, grabbed the tea chests and tossed them into a bonfire. Although the "Indians" were identified and brought to trial, they were found innocent. Maybe it helped that the sheriff was the brother of one of the accused and the jury foreman was the nephew of another.

All's well that ends well. Breathe deeply of the perfumed smoke if you're in the area in late December. You are smelling American history.

Ghost Tours on the Haunted Jersey Shore

A NUMBER OF NEW JERSEY SEASHORE CITIES AND TOWNS HAVE BEGUN offering "ghost tours," following the lead of New Orleans, where they have been a tradition for many years. Not every town offers actual "ghost tours," however, so you might want to consider planning your own to some of the unique locations that exist on or near the Jersey shore. Here are some suggestions.

Burlington County was once the home of Purgatory, a village no longer on the map. Atlantic County has a rural Route 666 that looks like just another country road by day, but no one willingly travels it at night. Then there are Hell's Kitchen, Double Trouble, and Bone Hill. Although you won't find Hell's Kitchen or Bone Hill on a modern New Jersey map, Double Trouble is located a few miles south of Toms River on the eastern coast.

For those who enjoy a more formal introduction to local haunts, Ocean City and Cape May give visitors the opportunity to "meet" some of the colorful characters who once lived in those shore communities. Ocean City's tour guides include a stop at the famous Flanders Hotel, a popular 1920s seaside establishment. Although most visitors rarely associate ghosts with the family resort, the Flanders has a resident spirit named Emily. Simon Lake, one of the town's founding fathers, is another ghost, who supposedly appears whenever there is any discussion about removing Ocean City's ban on alcohol.

Other towns often offer similar tours during the fall as a way of promoting local history. Another type of day trip that has become popular in recent years is the "cemetery tour," where hardy people troop to different graveyards to learn more about the lives of the people buried there—and perhaps see a ghostly sighting or two.

There are cemeteries from the northernmost reaches of the shore down to the southern seashore where local residents claim that spirits walk. Since dates and companies are changeable, it would be virtually impossible to offer a listing of all ghost tours here. If you are interested in visiting a particular area, we suggest you contact the local Chamber of Commerce or spend some time on the Internet for the latest information on regional folklore. Sites like www.hauntfinder.com and www.horrorfind.com offer a wide selection of "spirited" activities, ranging from the Hollowgraves Haunted Manor, open all summer at the Keansburg Amusement Park, to the Screaming Run Haunted Walk, held around Halloween at Leaming's Run Gardens in Swainton.

Be sure to check out the Haunted Cape May Tour (609-463-8984) at www.hauntednewjersey.com and the Ocean City Ghost Tour at www.ghosttour.com

Getting Weird on the Jersey Shore

ONE EXCELLENT RESOURCE FOR THE LATEST NEWS OF THE SUPERNATURAL is *Weird New Jersey*, a fascinating publication that began to pique the imagination of readers with tales of the supernatural in 1989, when it first appeared in newsletter form. Since that time, Mark Sceurman and Mark Moran, who describe themselves as the "publishers, editors, everything" of *WNJ*, have produced a book entitled *Weird New Jersey: Your Travel Guide to New Jersey's Local Legends and Best Kept Secrets* (New York: Barnes and Nobel, 2003). They followed it with *Weird U.S.: Your Travel Guide to America's Local Legends and Best Kept Secrets* (New York: Barnes and Nobel, 2004).

Weird New Jersey does an excellent job covering the paranormal in the Garden State. Many of the articles are sent in by readers who are audacious enough to explore the underground tunnels, abandoned sanitariums, and other unusual places in hope of sighting a spectral presence. *Weird New Jersey* plays a valuable role in documenting modern-day folk tales and keeping them alive for future generations. It can be found on the Internet at www.weirdnj.com or www.weird.us.com.

The Weird Wide Web

Anyone who has access to the Internet knows that you can find just about anything with a few keystrokes, regardless of the subject. If you are interested in learning more about the Jersey Shore's haunted history, there are thousands of sites devoted to the super-natural, ranging from contemporary and historical horror tales to practical advice on casting your own magical spells. Whether or not you do that voodoo, a number of them include stories about the paranormal in New Jersey and are ideal for the armchair adventurer who would rather not confront any ghosts or goblins first-hand. If you're interested in exploring, here are just a few stops on the Internet that are worth visiting:

American Society for Psychical Research
www.aspr.com

Ghostvillage.Com
www.ghostvillage.com

Lone Star Spirits Paranormal Investigations
www.lonestarspirits.org

New Jersey Ghost Hunters Society
www.njghs.net/pages/1/index.htm

Paranormal News
www.paranormalnews.com

Philadelphia Ghost Hunters Alliance
http://members.aol.com/Rayd8em

Real Haunted Houses
www.realhaunts.com

The Shadowlands
www.theshadowlands.net

South Jersey Ghost Research
http://southjerseyghostresearch.org/

Spiritsearchers
http://spiritsearchers.homestead.com/main.html

Bibliography

Barber, John, and Henry Howe. *Historical Collections of the State of New Jersey.* New York: S. Tuttle, 1844.

Beck, Henry Charlton. *Forgotten Towns of Southern New Jersey.* New Brunswick, NJ: Rutgers University Press, 1961.

———. *The Jersey Midlands.* New Brunswick, NJ: Rutgers University Press, 1962.

———. *The Roads of Home: Lanes and Legends of New Jersey.* New Brunswick, NJ: Rutgers University Press, 1956.

———. *Tales and Towns of Northern New Jersey.* New Brunswick, NJ: Rutgers University Press, 1964.

Boucher, Jack. *Absegami Yesteryear.* Egg Harbor City, NJ: Atlantic County Historical Society, 1963.

Burton, Hal. *Morro Castle.* New York: Viking Press, 1973.

Cohen, David Stephen. *The Folklore and Folklife of New Jersey.* New Brunswick, NJ: Rutgers University Press, 1984.

Federal Writers' Project. *New Jersey: A Guide to Its Present and Past.* New York: Viking Press, 1939.

Fernicola, Richard. *Twelve Days of Terror.* Guilford, CT: Lyons Press, 2001.

Heide, Robert, and John Gilman. *O' New Jersey: Daytripping, Back Roads, Eateries, and Funky Adventures.* New York: St. Martin's Press, 1992.

Kelly, Mike. *Fresh Jersey: Stories from an Altered State.* Philadelphia: Camino Books, 2000.

Kobbe, Gustav. *The Jersey Coast and Pines: An Illustrated Guide-Book with Road Maps.* 1889. Reprint, Baltimore: Gateway Press, 1970.

Mappen, Marc. *Jerseyana: The Underside of New Jersey History.* New Brunswick, NJ: Rutgers University Press, 1992.

Martinelli, Patricia, and Charles Stansfield. *Haunted New Jersey: Ghosts and Strange Phenomena of the Garden State.* Mechanicsburg, PA: Stackpole Books, 2004.

McCloy, James, and Ray Miller. *The Jersey Devil.* Moorestown, NJ: Middle Atlantic Press, 1976.

McMahon, William. *Pine Barrens Legends, Lore and Lies.* Wallingford, PA: The Middle Atlantic Press, 1980.

———. *South Jersey Towns: History and Legend.* New Brunswick, NJ: Rutgers University Press, 1973.

Pickering, David. *Casell Dictionary of Superstitions.* London: Casell, 1995.

Sceurman, Mark, and Mark Moran. *Weird New Jersey: Your Travel Guide to New Jersey's Local Legends and Best Kept Secrets.* New York: Barnes and Noble, 2003.

Skinner, Charles M. *American Myths and Legends.* Detroit: Gale Research Company, 1974.

Sommerville, George. *The Lure of Long Beach, New Jersey.* 1914. Reprint, Harvey Cedars, NJ: Down the Shore Publishing, 1987.

Stansfield, Charles. *Vacationing on the Jersey Shore: Guide to the Beach Resorts Past and Present.* Mechanicsburg, PA: Stackpole Books, 2004.

Stockton, Frank. *Stories of New Jersey.* New Brunswick, NJ: Rutgers University Press, 1991.

Waltzer, Jim, and Tom Wilk. *Tales of South Jersey: Profiles and Personalities.* New Brunswick, NJ: Rutgers University Press, 2001.

Weird NJ Magazine. Published twice a year, in May and October, by Weird NJ Inc., P.O. Box 1346, Bloomfield, NJ, 07003.

Wilson, Harold. *The Jersey Shore: A Social and Economic History of the Counties of Atlantic, Cape May, Monmouth and Ocean.* New York: Lewis Historical Publishing Company, 1953.

Acknowledgments

I WISH TO THANK MY EDITOR AND FRIEND, KYLE WEAVER, FOR HIS enthusiastic support, constant encouragement, and good advice. Amy Cooper, associate editor at Stackpole Books, did a superb job of editing—many thanks, Amy. The suitably haunting illustrations are the work of a talented young artist named Heather Adel Wiggins. My longtime friend and associate Laura Ruthig word-processed the manuscript and provided friendly encouragement throughout the project; I'm most grateful.

Many friends, colleagues, and even a few relatives shared their ghost stories, most on the grounds of anonymity. They know who they are and know how much I appreciate their confidence and assistance. My old friend and collaborator on a previous project, Patricia Martinelli, contributed some additional stories from her Internet research.

I am fortunate in being able to draw on the professional assistance and friendly advice of Rowan University's Campbell Library staff, especially MaryAnn Curtis Gonzales, and Joyce Olsen of the Stewart Collection. Rowan University's distinguished president, Dr. Donald Farish, who combines meticulous scholarship with visionary and inspirational leadership, has fostered an academic environment in which all forms of creative expression are encouraged. He may be a little surprised to see my current unconventional interest in this field of cultural geography and folklore sharing space on his bookshelf of faculty publications with my much more traditional geography textbooks.

As with many previous books, my dear wife, Diane
patiently endured my seemingly endless preoccupation with
ing and tolerated the presence of my untidy home office within
recreation room. I couldn't dream of a better soulmate; than
again, sweetheart.

About the Author

CHARLES ARTHUR STANSFIELD JR. HAS TAUGHT GEOGRAPHY AT ROWAN University for forty years. The study of geography and an interest in ghost stories might seem an unlikely combination. Stansfield has published a dozen textbooks on cultural and regional geography. In doing the research for his first general-interest nontextbook effort, a historical geography of the Jersey Shore titled *Vacationing on the Jersey Shore: Guide to the Beach Resorts Past and Present,* he came across some intriguing ghost stories set at the seashore. Ghost stories made only a brief appearance in that book, but they became the focus of *Haunted New Jersey: Ghosts and Strange Phenomena of the Garden State,* coauthored with Patricia Martinelli. After *Haunted New Jersey*'s publication, he continued to read and hear more ghost stories associated with the Jersey Shore and vicinity. This volume is the result, focusing on the seashore and vicinity in order to bring together the many tales of the supernatural that he could not include in his previous books.

Other Titles in the

Haunted Series

by Charles A. Stansfield Jr.

HAUNTED
MAINE
978-0-8117-3373-1

HAUNTED NEW JERSEY
with Patricia A. Martinelli
978-0-8117-3156-0

HAUNTED OHIO
978-0-8117-3472-1

HAUNTED VERMONT
978-0-8117-3399-1

WWW.STACKPOLEBOOKS.COM
1-800-732-3669

Other Titles in the
Haunted Series

HAUNTED CONNECTICUT
by Cheri Revai • 978-0-8117-3296-3

HAUNTED DELAWARE
by Patricia A. Martinelli • 978-0-8117-3297-0

HAUNTED FLORIDA
by Cynthia Thuman and Catherine Lower
978-0-8117-3498-6

HAUNTED GEORGIA
by Alan Brown • 978-0-8117-3443-1

HAUNTED ILLINOIS
by Troy Taylor • 978-0-8117-3499-4

HAUNTED MARYLAND
by Ed Okonowicz • 978-0-8117-3409-7

HAUNTED MASSACHUSETTS
by Cheri Revai • 978-0-8117-3221-5

HAUNTED NEW YORK
by Cheri Revai • 978-0-8117-3249-9

**HAUNTED
NEW YORK CITY**
by Cheri Revai • 978-0-8117-3471-4

HAUNTED PENNSYLVANIA
by Mark Nesbitt and Patty A. Wilson
978-0-8117-3298-7

HAUNTED TEXAS
by Alan Brown • 978-0-8117-3500-1

HAUNTED WEST VIRGINIA
by Patty A. Wilson • 978-0-8117-3400-4

WWW.STACKPOLEBOOKS.COM • 1-800-732-3669